KV-200-249

5th edition

Headway »»

Beginner Student's Book

Liz & John Soars • Jo McCaul

City and Islington College

BAT19702

OXFORD
UNIVERSITY PRESS

Contents

4   Contents

Go to **headwayonline.com** to download the Wordlist and full Audioscript.

Course overview

5th edition
Headway

Welcome to **Headway 5th edition**. Here's how the blended syllabus helps you link learning in the classroom with meaningful practice outside.

Student's Book

All the language and skills you need to improve your English, with grammar, vocabulary and skills work in every unit. Also available as an e-book.

Use your Student's Book in class with your teacher.

ACTIVITIES AUDIO VIDEO WORDLISTS

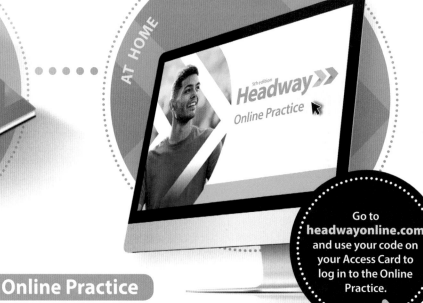

Go to **headwayonline.com** and use your code on your Access Card to log in to the Online Practice.

Workbook

Exclusive practice to match your Student's Book, unit by unit.

Use your Workbook for homework or for self-study to give you new input and practice.

Online Practice

Look again at Student's Book language you want to review or that you missed in class, do extra **Practice** activities, and **Check your Progress** on what you've learnt so far.

Use the Online Practice at home to extend your learning and get instant feedback on your progress.

headwayonline.com

Hello! 1

- Grammar *am/is/are*; *my/your*; This is ...; How are you?
- Vocabulary **What's this in English?; Numbers 1–10; Plurals**
- Everyday English **Good morning!**

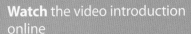 **Watch** the video introduction online

 Use your **Workbook** for self study

↪ **Go online** for more practice and to *Check your Progress*

What's your name?

🔊 **1.1** Read and listen. Say your name.

Hello, I'm Mara.

Hello, I'm Leo.

Hello, I'm Nari.

Grammar
am/is, my/your

1 🔊 **1.2** Read and listen.

Serena	Hello. I'm Serena. What's your name?
Tom	My name's Tom.
Serena	Hello, Tom.

2 🔊 **1.2** Listen again and repeat.

● **GRAMMAR SPOT**

I'm = I **am**
What's = What **is**
name's = name **is**

3 Stand up and practise.

Hello, I'm _____.
What's your name?

My name's _____.

Introductions

This is …

1 🔊 **1.3** Read and listen.

Serena	Tom, this is Carlos.
	Carlos, this is Tom.
Tom	Hello, Carlos.
Carlos	Hello, Tom.

🔊 **1.3** Listen again and repeat.

2 Practise in groups of three.

_____, this is _____.
_____, this is _____.

Hello, _____.

Hello, _____.

Nice to meet you

3 🔊 **1.4** Read and listen.

Paul	Hello. My name's Paul Bartosz.
Sarah	Hello. I'm Sarah Taylor. Nice to meet you.
Paul	Nice to meet you, too.

🔊 **1.4** Listen again and repeat.

4 Practise in pairs. Say your first name and your surname.

A Hello. My name's _____ _____.
B Hello. I'm _____ _____. Nice to meet you.
A Nice to meet you, too.

5 Choose a name. Stand up and say hello.

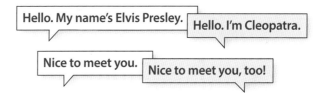

Hello. My name's Elvis Presley.

Hello. I'm Cleopatra.

Nice to meet you.

Nice to meet you, too!

How are you?

1 🔊 1.5 Read and listen.

1

Artur	Hi, Dinos. How are you?
Dinos	Fine, thanks, Artur. And you?
Artur	I'm OK, thanks.

2

Linda	Hello, May. How are you?
May	Very well, thank you. How are you?
Linda	Fine.

🔊 1.5 Listen again and repeat.

● GRAMMAR SPOT

Write '*m*, *is*, or *are*.

I _____ Helen.

How _____ you?

This _____ Tom.

➔ Grammar reference 1.1–1.3 ▶ p14

2 Answer your teacher.

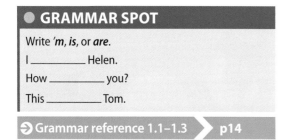

Hi, _____.
How are you?

Fine, thanks. And you?

Very well, thank you.

OK, thanks.

3 Stand up and practise.

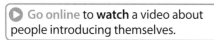 Go online to **watch** a video about
people introducing themselves.

Check it

4 Complete the conversations.

1

A Hello. _My_ name's Usha _____ your name?

B _____ _____ Ben.

2

A Shi, _____ is Huan.

B Hello, Huan.

C Hello, Shi. _____ to meet you.

3

A Hi, Sophie. How _____ you?

B Fine, thanks, Amy. And _____?

A _____ well, thanks.

➔ Go online for more **grammar** practice

Everyday English
Good morning!

1 Complete the conversations.

> Goodbye! Goodnight! ~~Good morning!~~ Good afternoon!

1
A _Good morning!_
B Good morning! What a lovely day!

2
A _____
B Hello. A cup of tea, please.

3
A _____ . Have a nice day!
B Bye! See you later, Mum!

4
A _____!
Sleep well.
B Night night, Daddy.

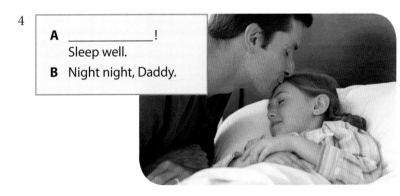

🔊 **1.6** Listen and check. Practise the conversations.

2 Put the words in the correct order.

1
A Good morning!

> are you How today

How are you today ?
B Fine, thanks. And you?

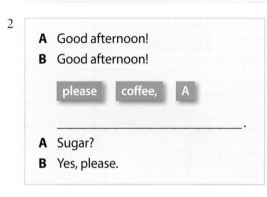

2
A Good afternoon!
B Good afternoon!

> please coffee, A

_____ .
A Sugar?
B Yes, please.

3
A Goodbye!

> nice Have day a

_____ .
B Thank you. And you.

> you later See

_____ .

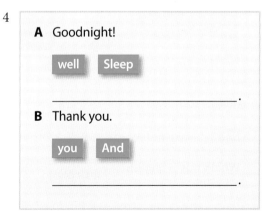

4
A Goodnight!

> well Sleep

_____ .
B Thank you.

> you And

_____ .

🔊 **1.7** Listen and check. Practise the conversations.

🔗 Go online for more **speaking** practice

Vocabulary and speaking
What's this in English?

1 Write the words.

 1

 2

 3

 4

 5

a bus

an apple

a phone

a laptop

an umbrella

a bike

a house

a bag

a watch

a book

a photo

a sandwich

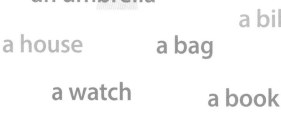 6

 8

 7

 9

 10

 11

 12

2 🔊 **1.8** Listen and repeat the words.

3 🔊 **1.9** Listen and repeat.

What's this in English? It's a photo.

4 Work with a partner. Point to a photo. Ask and answer questions.

What's this in English? It's a watch.

What's this in English? It's an apple.

5 Point to things in the room. Ask your teacher.

What's this in English? It's a/an ....

● **GRAMMAR SPOT**

1 It's = It is
2 **a** book   **an** apple
  a watch   **an** umbrella

➔ Grammar reference 1.4   ▸ p14

Numbers 1–10 and plurals

1 🔊 1.10 Read and listen. Practise the numbers.

1 one

2 two

3 three

4 four

5 five

6 six

7 seven

8 eight

9 nine

10 ten

2 Say the numbers round the class.

3 Write the numbers.

 1 *five* books

 2 _____ bikes

 3 _____ houses

 4 _____ umbrellas

 5 _____ photos

 6 _____ laptops

7 _____ watches

8 _____ apples

 9 _____ sandwiches

🔊 1.11 Listen and check.

4 🔊 1.12 Listen and repeat.

/s/	/z/	/ɪz/
books	apples	buses
bikes	bags	houses
laptops	phones	watches
	photos	sandwiches
	umbrellas	

5 Ask and answer questions.

What's in 3?   Eight houses.

● GRAMMAR SPOT

Singular	Plural
one book	two books
one bus	two buses

➔ Grammar reference 1.5   p14

📲 Go online for more **vocabulary** practice

Grammar reference

➔ 1.1 am/are/is

I	'm / am	Serena.
You	're / are	Tom.
My name	's / is	James Bond.
This	is	Paul Bartosz.

➔ 1.2 Questions with question words

What's your name?
(what's = what is)

What's this in English?
How are you?

➔ 1.3 Possessive adjectives

My name's John.
What's **your** name?

➔ 1.4 a/an

We use *an* before words that begin with *a, e, i, o* or *u*.

an apple
an umbrella
an English book

but:

a bike
a phone
a house

➔ 1.5 Plural nouns

1 Most nouns add -*s*.

book	→	book**s**
phone	→	phone**s**
laptop	→	laptop**s**

2 Some nouns add -*es*.

sandwich	→	sandwich**es**
bus	→	bus**es**
watch	→	watch**es**

Wordlist

adj = adjective   *det* = determiner   *prep* = preposition
adv = adverb   *excl* = exclamation   *pron* = pronoun
conj = conjunction   *n* = noun   *v* = verb

a cup of tea /ə ˌkʌp əv ˈtiː/ _____
and *conj* /ænd/, /ənd/ _____
apple *n* /ˈæpl/ _____
bag *n* /bæg/ _____
bike *n* /baɪk/ _____
book *n* /bʊk/ _____
bus *n* /bʌs/ _____
Bye! *excl* /baɪ/ _____
coffee *n* /ˈkɒfi/ _____
Daddy *n* /ˈdædi/ _____
day *n* /deɪ/ _____
English *n* /ˈɪŋglɪʃ/ _____
fine *adj* /faɪn/ _____
first name *n* /ˈfɜːst ˌneɪm/ _____
Good afternoon! *excl* /gʊd ˌɑːftəˈnuːn/ _____
Good morning! *excl* /ˌgʊd ˈmɔːnɪŋ/ _____
Good night! *excl* /gʊdˈnaɪt/ _____
Goodbye! *excl* /gʊdˈbaɪ/ _____
Have a nice day! /ˌhæv ə naɪs ˈdeɪ/ _____
Hello! *excl* /həˈləʊ/ _____
house *n* /haʊs/ _____
How are you? /ˌhaʊ ə ˈjuː/ _____
laptop *n* /ˈlæptɒp/ _____
lovely *adj* /ˈlʌvli/ _____
Mum *n* /mʌm/ _____
name *n* /neɪm/ _____
Nice to meet you. /ˌnaɪs tə ˈmiːt ju/ _____
OK *adj* /ˌəʊ ˈkeɪ/ _____
phone *n* /fəʊn/ _____
photo *n* /ˈfəʊtəʊ/ _____
please *excl* /pliːz/ _____
sandwich *n* /ˈsænwɪtʃ/ _____
See you later! *excl* /ˌsiː ju ˈleɪtə(r)/ _____
Sleep well! *excl* /ˈsliːp ˌwel/ _____
sugar *n* /ˈʃʊgə(r)/ _____
surname *n* /ˈsɜːneɪm/ _____
Thank you *excl* /ˈθæŋkjuː/ _____
Thanks *excl* /θæŋks/ _____
this *pron* /ˈðɪs/ _____
today *adv* /təˈdeɪ/ _____
umbrella *n* /ʌmˈbrelə/ _____
very well /ˌveri ˈwel/ _____
watch *n* /wɒtʃ/ _____
What? *pron* /ˌwɒt/ _____
with *prep* /wɪð/ _____
your *det* /jɔː(r)/ _____

Numbers 1–10

one /wʌn/ _____
two /tuː/ _____
three /θriː/ _____
four /fɔː(r)/ _____
five /faɪv/ _____
six /sɪks/ _____
seven /ˈsevn/ _____
eight /eɪt/ _____
nine /naɪn/ _____
ten /ten/ _____

Your world 2

- Grammar *he/she/they; his/her;*
  Questions – Where's she from?
- Vocabulary **Countries; Adjectives**

- Everyday English **Numbers 11–30**
- Reading **A holiday in New York**

The Earth and the Moon

1 Match the countries below to the flags.
Canada Australia the US the UK England Scotland

2 Work with a partner. Compare your answers.

a b

c d

e f

 Watch the video introduction online

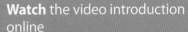 Use your **Workbook** for self study

 Go online for more practice and to *Check your Progress*

She's from China

STARTER

Find your country on the map on page 17. Find these countries on the map.

Argentina	Australia	Brazil	Canada	China	England	Egypt
France	Italy	Japan	Spain	Russia	Turkey	the US

🔊 **2.1** Listen and repeat.

📤 Go online for more **vocabulary** practice

Grammar *he/she, his/her*

1 🔊 **2.2** Read and listen.

Antonio	Hello, I'm Antonio. What's your name?
Nuwa	My name's Nuwa.
Antonio	Where are you from, Nuwa?
Nuwa	I'm from China. Where are you from?
Antonio	I'm from Italy. From Milan.

🔊 **2.2** Listen again and repeat.

2 Where are you from? Stand up and practise.

> **Where are you from?**

> **I'm from Spain/Turkey ...**
> **Where ... ?**

3 🔊 **2.3** Read, listen and repeat.

His name's Antonio. He's from Italy.

Her name's Nuwa. She's from China.

● **GRAMMAR SPOT**

1 he's = he is
  she's = she is

2 Put the pronouns in the correct box.

he she his her

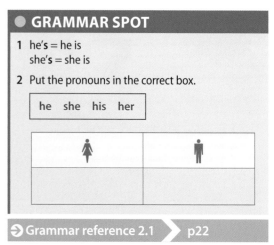

➔ **Grammar reference 2.1** ▸ p22

16   Unit 2 • Your world

Questions

1 Complete the sentences about the people.

Her name's Julie.
She's _from_ _England_.

_____ name's Nadia.
She's _____ _____.

_____ name's Anton.
He's _____ _____.

_____ name's Geoff.
He's _____ _____.

_____ name's Paula.
She's _____ _____.

_____ name's Amun.
He's _____ _____.

_____ name's Lan.
She's _____ _____.

_____ name's Oliver.
He's _____ _____.

2.4 Listen and check. Repeat the sentences.

2 **2.5** Listen and repeat the questions.

What's his name?	Where's he from?
What's her name?	Where's she from?

3 Ask and answer questions about the people in the photos on the map.

What's his name?
His name's Geoff.

Where's he from?
He's from Canada.

● GRAMMAR SPOT

1 Where's = Where is

2 Complete the questions with *is* or *are*.

Where _____ she from?

Where _____ he from?

Where _____ you from?

→ Grammar reference 2.2   p22

Practice

Cities and countries

1 Where are the cities? Ask and answer.

Venice	Australia
New York	France
Moscow	Russia
Paris	the US
Beijing	Turkey
Sydney	Brazil
Rio de Janeiro	Italy
Istanbul	China

> Where's Venice? It's in Italy.

> Where's Moscow? It's in Russia.

🔊 **2.6** Listen and check.

2 Work with a partner.

> Student A Look at the photos on this page.

> Student B Look at the photos on p141.

Ask and answer questions to complete the information.

> What's her name? Her name's …

> Where's she from? She's from …

Talking about you

3 Ask about the students in the class.

> What's his name? His name's Marco.

> Where's he from? He's from Rome.

> What's her name? Her name's Donatella.

> Where's she from? She's from Rome, too.

Student A

1
Her name's …
She's …

2
_____

3
_____

4
_____

Student B

5
His name's Fabio.
He's from Venice.

6
Her name's Mia.
She's from Sydney.

7
His name's Slava.
He's from Moscow.

8
Her name's Suyin.
She's from Beijing.

Questions and answers

4 🔊 **2.7** Listen and complete the conversation. Practise it.

> **Blanca**   Hello, I'm Blanca. What's ¹_____ name?
> **Rafael**   ²_____ name's Rafael.
> **B**   Hello, Rafael. Where are you ³_____?
> **R**   ⁴_____ from Spain. Where are you from?
> **B**   Oh, I'm from Spain, too. ⁵_____ _____ Barcelona.
> **R**   Really? I'm from Barcelona, too!
> **B**   Oh, nice to meet you, Rafael.

5 🔊 **2.8** Listen and write the countries.

1 Mateo: *Argentina*   3 Charles: _____
  Akemi: _____   Bud: _____

2 Loretta and Jason:
_____

6 Match the questions and answers.

1	_h_ Where are you from?	a	His name's Edvin.
2	___ What's her name?	b	It's a laptop.
3	___ What's his name?	c	Fine, thanks. And you?
4	___ Where's he from?	d	It's in England.
5	___ What's this in English?	e	My name's Rachna.
6	___ How are you?	f	He's from France.
7	___ Where's Liverpool?	g	Her name's Sophie.
8	___ What's your name?	h	I'm from China.

🔊 **2.9** Listen and check.

Work with a partner. Take turns to ask and answer the questions.

Check it

7 Tick (✓) the correct sentence.

1 ☐ My name Goran.
  ✓ My name's Goran.

2 ☐ What's he's name?
  ☐ What's his name?

3 ☐ 'What's his name?' 'Rosa'.
  ☐ 'What's her name?' 'Rosa'.

4 ☐ He's from Japan.
  ☐ His from Japan.

5 ☐ Where she from?
  ☐ Where's she from?

6 ☐ What's her name?
  ☐ What's she name?

> ↪ Go online for more **grammar** practice

Reading and vocabulary
A holiday in New York

1 🔊 2.10 Read and listen.

This is a photo of **Claude** and **Holly Duval** from Montreal in Canada. They are on holiday in New York City. Holly is from Canada and Claude is from France. They are married. Holly is an architect. Her office is in the centre of Montreal. Claude is a doctor. His hospital is in the centre of Montreal, too.

2 Complete the sentences.

1 Holly is from *Montreal* in Canada.
2 She's an _____ .
3 Her _____ is in the centre of Montreal.
4 Claude is from _____ .
5 He's a _____ .
6 His hospital is in the _____ of Montreal, too.
7 They are on _____ in New York.
8 They _____ married.

3 Complete the questions about Claude and Holly. Ask and answer with a partner.

What's ... name?   Where ... office?

Where ... from?   Where ... hospital?

● GRAMMAR SPOT

Write *is ('s)* or *are ('re)*.

You _____ a teacher.
She _____ an architect.
He _____ a doctor.
They _____ from Montreal.

➔ Grammar reference 2.3   ▸ p22

4 🔊 2.11 Listen to Claude and Holly. Complete the conversations.

1

~~weather~~   awful

C Oh no! Look at the _weather_ !
H Ugh! It's _____ .

2

hamburger   really good

H Mmm. Look at my _____ ! It looks great!
C My pizza is _____ , too!

3

amazing   ~~building~~

C Wow! This _building_ is fantastic!
H Yes, you're right. It's _____ .
The Freedom Tower is my favourite building in New York now.

4

beautiful   Look

C Wow! _____ at the view!
H It's _____ .

🔊 2.11 Listen again and check.
Practise the conversations.

▶ Go online to **watch** a video about different cities and countries.

Everyday English
Numbers 11–30

1 Say the numbers 1–10 round the class.

2 🔊 2.12 Listen, read and repeat.

11	**12**	**13**	**14**	**15**
eleven	twelve	thirteen	fourteen	fifteen

16	**17**	**18**	**19**	**20**
sixteen	seventeen	eighteen	nineteen	twenty

3 Say the numbers 1–20 round the class.

4 Write the numbers your teacher says.
Say the numbers your teacher writes.

5 Match the numbers.

21	twenty-five
22	twenty-seven
23	twenty-one
24	twenty-eight
25	twenty-two
26	twenty-four
27	twenty-nine
28	twenty-three
29	thirty
30	twenty-six

🔊 2.13 Listen and repeat. Say the numbers 1–30 round the class.

6 🔊 2.14 Listen and tick (✓) the numbers you hear.

1 **22** **12** ✓ **10** **20**
2 **17** **15** **16** **14**
3 **21** **29** **19** **9**
4 **11** **7** **17** **27**
5 **23** **3** **13** **30**

7 Look at the photos. How old is he/she?

> I think he's about 26.

> I think he's 30.

🔊 2.15 Listen and find out.

↪ Go online for more **speaking** practice

Grammar reference

⊃ 2.1 Possessive adjectives

My name's Serena.
What's **your** name?
His name's Antonio.
What's **her** name?

❶ his = possessive adjective
his name, **his** bike, **his** watch

he's = he is
He's Bruno. **He's** from Brazil. **He's** fine.

⊃ 2.2 Questions with question words

Where	are you	from?
	is she	
	is he	
What	's this (is this)	in English?

How old	are you?	I'm 27.
	is he?	He's 18.
	is she?	She's 12.

⊃ 2.3 am/are/is

I'm (I am)	
You're (You are)	from England.
	a student.
He's (He is)	
She's (She is)	
It's (It is)	a laptop.
They're (They are)	in New York.
	married.

Wordlist

adj = adjective	det = determiner	pl = plural
adv = adverb	n = noun	pron = pronoun
conj = conjunction	phr = phrase	v = verb

amazing	adj	/ə'meɪzɪŋ/	_____
architect	n	/'ɑːkɪtekt/	_____
awful	adj	/'ɔːfl/	_____
beautiful	adj	/'bjuːtɪfl/	_____
building	n	/'bɪldɪŋ/	_____
centre	n	/'sentə(r)/	_____
city	n	/'sɪti/	_____
country	n	/'kʌntri/	_____
doctor	n	/'dɒktə(r)/	_____
fantastic	adj	/fæn'tæstɪk/	_____
favourite	adj	/'feɪvərɪt/	_____
great	adj	/greɪt/	_____
hamburger	n	/'hæmbɜːgə(r)/	_____
hospital	n	/'hɒspɪtl/	_____
map	n	/mæp/	_____
married	adj	/'mærid/	_____
office	n	/'ɒfɪs/	_____
on holiday	phr	/ɒn 'hɒlədeɪ/	_____
really good	adj	/ˌriːəli 'gʊd/	_____
too	adv	/tuː/	_____
view	n	/vjuː/	_____
weather	n	/'weðə(r)/	_____
Where?	adv	/weə(r)/	_____
world	n	/wɜːld/	_____
You're right.		/jɔːr 'raɪt/	_____

Countries

Argentina	n	/ˌɑːdʒən'tiːnə/	_____
Australia	n	/ɒ'streɪliə/	_____
Brazil	n	/brə'zɪl/	_____
Canada	n	/'kænədə/	_____
China	n	/'tʃaɪnə/	_____
Egypt	n	/'iːdʒɪpt/	_____
England	n	/'ɪŋglənd/	_____
France	n	/frɑːns/	_____
Italy	n	/'ɪtəli/	_____
Japan	n	/dʒə'pæn/	_____
Russia	n	/'rʌʃə/	_____
Scotland	n	/'skɒtlənd/	_____
Spain	n	/speɪn/	_____
the UK	n	/ðə ˌjuː 'keɪ/	_____
the US	n	/ðə ˌjuː 'es/	_____
Turkey	n	/'tɜːki/	_____

Numbers 11–30

eleven	/ɪ'levn/	_____
twelve	/twelv/	_____
thirteen	/θɜː'tiːn/	_____
fourteen	/fɔː'tiːn/	_____
fifteen	/fɪf'tiːn/	_____
sixteen	/sɪks'tiːn/	_____
seventeen	/sevn'tiːn/	_____
eighteen	/eɪ'tiːn/	_____
nineteen	/naɪn'tiːn/	_____
twenty	/'twenti/	_____
twenty-one	/ˌtwenti'wʌn/	_____
twenty-two	/ˌtwenti'tuː/	_____
twenty-three	/ˌtwenti'θriː/	_____
…		
thirty	/'θɜːti/	_____

All about you 3

- Grammar **Negatives – *'m not/isn't/aren't*; Questions and answers; *we/they are/aren't***
- Vocabulary **Jobs**
- Everyday English **Social expressions (1)**
- Reading **We're in Paris**

1 3.1 Read the questions and answers. Listen and repeat.

1 What's your name?
My name's Jordan.

2 Where are you from?
I'm from the US.

3 What's your job?
I'm a teacher.

2 Ask and answer the questions with a partner.

Watch the video introduction online

Use your **Workbook** for self study

Go online for more practice and to *Check your Progress*

What's his job?

1 Match the jobs and the photos.

| a teacher   a police officer   a taxi driver   a builder |
| a receptionist   ~~a businessman~~   a nurse   an architect |

1 a businessman

2

3

4

5

6

7

8

🔊 **3.2** Listen and repeat.

2 🔊 **3.3** Listen to the questions and answers and repeat.

| What's his job? | He's a businessman. | ❓ |
| What's her job? | She's an architect. | |

3 Look at the photos in exercise 1. Ask and answer the questions with a partner.

4 What's your job? Ask and answer.

> What's your job?

I'm a student.

I'm a builder.

📲 Go online for more **vocabulary** practice

Grammar

Negatives – *he/she isn't*

1 **3.4** Look at Sunil and Dana. Listen and repeat.

Sunil Teacher? Student?

He isn't a teacher. He's a student.

Dana Nurse? Doctor?

She isn't a nurse. She's a doctor.

2 Look at photos 1–8 on page 24 again. Make more positive and negative sentences.

He/She isn't a … **He/She's a …**

● GRAMMAR SPOT

He**'s** a student. **'s** = is

She **isn't** a nurse. **isn't** = is not

Questions and answers

Personal information

1 Read about Adam.

ID card

Surname:	Clarke
First name:	Adam
Country:	England
Address:	37 Kings Street, Manchester, M12 4JB
Phone:	07700 955031
Age:	27
Job:	Police Officer
Married:	No

Adam Clarke

2 Complete the questions and answers.

1 What's his _surname____?   Clarke.
2 What's his _____ _____?   Adam.
3 Where's he _____?   England.
4 What's his _____?   37 Kings Street, Manchester, M12 4JB.
5 What's his _____ number?   07700 955031.
6 How old is he?   He's _____ .
7 What's his _____?   He's a police officer.
8 Is he _____ ?   No, he isn't.

3.5 Listen and check. Practise the questions and answers with a partner.

3 **3.6** Read and listen. Then listen again and repeat.

Is Adam from Australia? ✗ No, he isn't.
Is he from Canada? ✗ No, he isn't.
Is he from England? ✓ Yes, he is.

4 Ask and answer the questions about Adam.

1 Is he from … *London? Oxford? Manchester?*
2 Is he … *19? 24? 27?*
3 Is he a … *teacher? doctor? police officer?*
4 Is he married?

Check it

5 Complete the sentences.

1 Adam *isn't* from Australia. He**'s** from England.
2 His phone number ____ 07700 955032. It____ 07700 955031.
3 He____ 30. He____ 27.
4 He____ married.

▶ Go online to **watch** a video about a woman called Paula Harrid.

Negatives – *I'm not, they/we aren't*

The 5-a-side football team

1 Look at the picture. Who are the people?

2 🔊 **3.7** Read and listen to the interview with the girls.

3 🔊 **3.7** Listen again and complete the questions and answers in the interview.

4 Answer the questions about the team.
   1 What's the team's name?
   2 Are Shona and Gillian sisters?
   3 Are they from England?
   4 Are all the girls teachers?
   5 Is Shona the best football player?
   6 Are they all really good footballers?

   🔊 **3.8** Listen and check. Practise the questions and answers.

Fiona   Gillian   Kate

The UK

SCOTLAND

NORTHERN IRELAND

WALES   ENGLAND

Shona   Emma

GRAMMAR SPOT

1 **Negative**

I'm not a nurse.	**I'm not** = I am not.
They aren't from England.	**They aren't** = They are not.
We aren't teachers.	**We aren't** = We are not.

2 **Short answers**

Are you from Glasgow?	Yes, I am./No, I'm not.
	Yes, we are./No, we aren't.
Is this your football team?	Yes, it is./No, it isn't.
Are they from England?	Yes, they are./No, they aren't.

➔ **Grammar reference 3.1–3.2**   **p30**

---

5 Practise the interview in groups of three.

Talking about you

6 Work with a partner. Ask and answer the questions about you.

Are you from Scotland?

Are you an architect?   No ...

Are you a taxi driver?   Yes ...

Are you married?

An interview with

🏐 Scottish Rovers

I Good afternoon. ¹ *Is this* your 5-a-side football team?

G Yes, it is.

I So, ² _____ _____ the Scottish Rovers?

All Yes, we are!

I Nice to meet you all. And ³ _____ _____ the captain, Shona Robertson?

G No, I'm not. I'm Gillian Robertson. This ⁴ _____ Shona. She's my sister.

I Ahh, sorry. Hi, Shona. So you're the captain.

S Yes, I ⁵ _____ . Hi!

I And you're a nurse, right?

S No. I'm not a nurse, I'm a teacher.

I Oh. OK. Sorry. And where ⁶ _____ you and your sister from?

S & G We're from Glasgow.

I I see. ⁷ _____ _____ both teachers?

S No, we aren't. Gillian's a student doctor.

G That's right.

I And the other girls? ⁸ _____ _____ all students?

G No, they aren't. Fiona and Kate are students, but Emma is a receptionist.

I I see. Interesting. OK, Shona, you're the captain so, ⁹ _____ _____ the best footballer in the team?

S No, I'm not. We're all really good footballers.

I I'm sure you are. Well, lovely to meet you all. Good luck in the final in Paris.

Practice

Is he a taxi driver?

1 Look at the pictures of Diego and Isabella. Where are they?

2 ◆)) 3.9 Listen to the conversations. Complete the chart.

First name	Diego	Isabella
Surname	Hernandez	Blanco
Country	Mexico	
City/Town		
Phone number		08842 666455
Age	42	
Job		waitress
Married		

◆)) 3.9 Listen again and check.

3 Ask and answer the questions with a partner.

> Is **Diego** from Mexico? *Yes, he is.*
> Is he a police officer?
> Is he 30?
> Is he married?

> Is **Isabella** from Brazil?
> Is she a receptionist?
> Is she 29?
> Is she married?

4 Talk about Diego and Isabella.

> Diego is a taxi driver. He's from …

> Isabella is a waitress. Her surname is …

Talking about you

5 Complete the questions.

1 *What's your* first name?
2 _____ _____ surname?
3 _____ _____ you from?
4 _____ _____ phone number?
5 How old _____ _____ ?
6 _____ _____ job?
7 _____ _____ married?

In groups, ask and answer the questions.

Writing

6 Write about another student. Read it aloud.

Her first name's …   Her surname's …   Her phone number is …

Check it

7 Tick (✓) the correct sentence.

1 ☐ She's name's Maria.
  ✓ Her name's Maria.

2 ☐ His job is an architect.
  ☐ He's an architect.

3 ☐ We aren't sisters.
  ☐ We's not sisters.

4 ☐ I'm not a doctor.
  ☐ I aren't a doctor.

5 ☐ They isn't from Spain.
  ☐ They aren't from Spain.

6 ☐ She isn't married.
  ☐ She not married.

Reading and listening
We're in Paris!

1 Read the newspaper article about the football team, *Scottish Rovers*.

Scottish Rovers in Paris

Scottish team in football final

The five-a-side football team, *Scottish Rovers*, are in the final in Paris. The team from Scotland are in the European final!

They are all from Glasgow. Two of the girls, Shona and Gillian Robertson, are sisters. Shona is the captain of the team.

'We are so happy we're in Paris' says Shona, 'Paris is beautiful and the Eiffel Tower is amazing!'

The final is tomorrow and the girls are very excited. 'We're all fine' says Gillian. 'We aren't nervous at all! It's great to be in the final and it's fantastic to be in Paris.'

Today it's coffee time in a French café. Tomorrow they play *Atletico Bilbao* from Spain in the final!

2 Answer the questions.

1 Where are the girls?
2 Is it the world final?
3 When is the final?
4 Are they nervous or excited?

3 Read about the team again. Correct the information.

1 Scottish Rovers are in Italy.
They aren't in Italy. They're in France .
2 Shona is from England.
_____ .
3 Gillian is the captain.
_____ .
4 The final is today.
_____ .
5 They're in a hotel in Paris now.
_____ .

🔊 **3.10** Listen and check. Practise the lines.

● **GRAMMAR SPOT**

We're in Paris.   **we're** = we are

Interview with the team

4 🔊 **3.11** Listen to the interview with the girls and answer the questions.

1 Is it the team's first time in Paris?
2 How old are Kate, Fiona and Emma?
3 How old are the twins?
4 Are the twins both married?
5 Who is Tom? What's his job?

5 🔊 **3.11** Look at audioscript 3.11 on page 142. Read and listen to the interview.

Roleplay

6 Work in groups of four. You are a sports team.

• What's your sport?
• What's the name of the team?
• What are your names?
• Where are you from?
• How old are you?
• What are your jobs?

Ask and answer the questions with another group.

⬆ Go online for more **grammar** practice

Everyday English
Social expressions (1)

1 🔊 3.12 Listen and look at the photos.

2 Complete the conversations with the words in the boxes.

OK	sorry	problem

A I'm so *sorry*.

B That's _____ . No
   _____ .

Thanks	please

C A black coffee, _____ .

D That's £2.40.

C _____ very much.

Excuse	don't know

E _____ me! Where's the station?

F I'm sorry. I _____ .

kind	welcome	very much

G Thank you _____ . That's very _____ .

H You're _____ .

don't understand	sorry

I ¿Qué hora es?

J I'm _____ . I _____ .

over there	Thanks a lot	Excuse

K _____ me!
   Where are the toilets?

L They're _____ .

K _____ .

🔊 3.12 Listen again and check.

3 Work with a partner. Practise the conversations. Stand up and act out the conversations.

[Go online for more **speaking** practice

Grammar reference

→ 3.1 Negatives, questions and short answers

Negative

I	**'m not** (am not)	a teacher.
He She	**isn't** (is not)	from Spain. married.
We They	**aren't** (are not)	very well.

Yes/No **questions and short answers**

Are you married?	Yes, I **am**. No, I **'m not**.
Is he/she a teacher?	Yes, he/she **is**. No, he/she **isn't**.
Is her name Alice?	Yes, it **is**. No, it **isn't**.
Are they English?	Yes, they **are**. No, they **aren't**.

→ 3.2 Verb *to be*

Positive

I	**'m** (am)	
He She It	**'s** (is)	from the US.
You We They	**'re** (are)	

Negative

I	**'m not**	
He She It	**isn't**	English.
You We They	**aren't**	

Questions with question words

What	**is** your name? **is** her address? **is** his phone number?
Where	**are** you from? **is** he from? **are** they from?
How old	**are** you? **are** they?

Answers

John Mason. 16, Albert Road, Bristol. 01693 456729.
From Spain.
I'm 16. They're six and ten.

Yes/No **questions**

Is	he she it	American?
Are	you we they	married?

Short answers

Yes, he **is**. No, she **isn't**. Yes, it **is**.
Yes, I **am**. No, we **aren't**. No, they **aren't**.

Wordlist

adj = adjective	*det* = determiner	*pl* = plural
adv = adverb	*excl* = exclamation	*pron* = pronoun
conj = conjunction	*n* = noun	*v* = verb

address   *n* /ə'dres/   _____
age   *n* /eɪdʒ/   _____
all   *adv* /ɔːl/   _____
best   *adj* /best/   _____
both   *det* /bəʊθ/   _____
builder   *n* /'bɪldə(r)/   _____
bus driver   *n* /'bʌs ˌdraɪvə(r)/   _____
businessman   *n* /'bɪznəsmæn/   _____
captain   *n* /'kæptɪn/   _____
café   *n* /'kæfeɪ/   _____
excited   *adj* /ɪk'saɪtɪd/   _____
Excuse me!   *excl* /ɪk'skjuːz ˌmiː/   _____
final   *n* /'faɪnl/   _____
first time   /fɜːst 'taɪm/   _____
footballer   *n* /'fʊtbɔːlə(r)/   _____
football player   *n* /'fʊtbɔːl ˌpleɪə(r)/   _____
football team   *n* /'fʊtbɔːl tiːm/   _____
forty   /'fɔːti/   _____
girl   *n* /gɜːl/   _____
Good luck!   *excl* /gʊd 'lʌk/   _____
happy   *adj* /'hæpi/   _____
here   *adv* /hɪə(r)/   _____
Hi   *excl* /haɪ/   _____
hotel   *n* /həʊ'tel/   _____
I don't know   *phr* /aɪ ˌdəʊnt 'nəʊ/   _____
I don't understand   *phr* /aɪ ˌdəʊnt ʌndə'stænd/   _____
I'm sorry   *phr* /aɪm 'sɒri/   _____
I'm sure.   *phr* /aɪm 'ʃɔː(r)/   _____
I see.   *phr* /aɪ 'siː/   _____
interesting   *adj* /'ɪntrəstɪŋ/   _____
interview   *n* /'ɪntəvjuː/   _____
job   *n* /dʒɒb/   _____
nervous   *adj* /'nɜːvəs/   _____
no problem   *phr* /'nəʊ prɒbləm/   _____
now   *adv* /naʊ/   _____
nurse   *n* /nɜːs/   _____
other   *adj* /'ʌðə(r)/   _____
over there   *adv* /ˌəʊvə 'ðeə/   _____
personal information   *n* /ˌpɜːsənl ɪnfə'meɪʃn/   _____
phone number   *n* /'fəʊn ˌnʌmbə(r)/   _____
police officer   *n* /pə'liːs ˌɒfɪsə(r)/   _____
receptionist   *n* /rɪ'sepʃənɪst/   _____
Right?   *excl* /raɪt/   _____
sister   *n* /'sɪstə(r)/   _____
station   *n* /'steɪʃn/   _____
student   *n* /'stjuːdnt/   _____
taxi driver   *n* /'tæksi ˌdraɪvə(r)/   _____
teacher   *n* /'tiːtʃə(r)/   _____
That's right.   *phr* /ðæts 'raɪt/   _____
toilet   *n* /'tɔɪlət/   _____
tomorrow   *adv* /tə'mɒrəʊ/   _____
twin   *n* /twɪn/   _____
very   *adj* /'veri/   _____
waitress   *n* /'weɪtrəs/   _____
well   *excl* /wel/   _____

Family and friends

4

1 🔊 4.1 Look at the family tree. Listen to the description.

```
Pablo ──────── Gina
        │
  Bruno    Nina
```

2 Work with a partner. Describe the family tree.
Her name's Nina and …

 Watch the video introduction online

 Use your **Workbook** for self study

 Go online for more practice and to *Check your Progress*

My family

1 Complete the chart.

I	you	he	she	we	they
my				*our*	*their*

2 Talk about things in the classroom.

> This is my bag.
> This is her book.
> This is our class.

Grammar
Possessive 's

1 🔊 4.2 Read and listen.

IAN McCAUL

This is Ian McCaul. He's married and this is his family. Their house is in Belfast, in Northern Ireland. He's a head teacher. Ian's school is in the centre of town.

Jenny is Ian's wife. She's a nurse. Her hospital is in the centre of town, too.

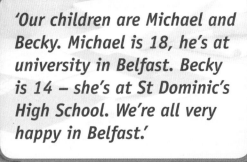

'Our children are Michael and Becky. Michael is 18, he's at university in Belfast. Becky is 14 – she's at St Dominic's High School. We're all very happy in Belfast.'

GRAMMAR SPOT

1 He**'s** married.   He**'s** a head teacher.   **'s = is**
2 This is Ian**'s** family.   **'s** = the family of Ian
   This is his family.
3 Ian's
   his   school   her   hospital
                            Jenny's

➜ **Grammar reference 4.1–4.2** ▶ **p40**

2 Answer the questions.

1 Is Ian married?
   Yes, he is   .
2 Where's their house?
   _____ .
3 What's Ian's job?
   _____ .
4 Where's his school?
   _____ .
5 What's Jenny's job?
   _____ .
6 Are their children both at school?
   _____ .

🔊 **4.3** Listen, check and practise.

Vocabulary
Who are they?

3 🔊 **4.4** Listen and repeat.

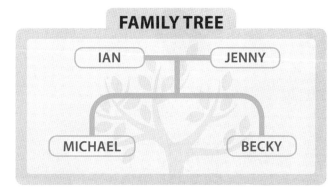

👩	mother	daughter	sister	wife
👨	father	son	brother	husband
👩👨	parents	children		

4 Look at the family tree.

FAMILY TREE

IAN ——— JENNY

MICHAEL   BECKY

🔊 **4.5** Listen and complete the sentences.

1 Jenny is Ian's _wife_.
2 Ian is Jenny's _____.
3 Becky is Jenny and Ian's _____.
4 Michael is Jenny and Ian's _____.
5 Ian is Becky's _____.
6 Jenny is Michael's _____.
7 Becky is Michael's _____.
8 Michael is Becky's _____.
9 Jenny and Ian are Michael and Becky's _____.
10 Michael and Becky are Jenny and Ian's _____.

🔊 **4.5** Listen again and check.

5 Work with a partner. Ask and answer questions about Ian's family.

Who's Michael?   He's Becky's brother.
                 He's Jenny's son.

6 🔊 **4.6** Listen to the McCaul family. Who is speaking?

1 *Jenny*   4 _____
2 _____   5 _____
3 _____

📲 Go online for more **vocabulary** practice

Practice

An Australian family

1 🔊 **4.7** Listen to Darren Marinos from Sydney. Complete the information about his family.

	Name	Age	Job
Darren's sister	*Elina*		
Darren's mother			
Darren's father			

2 Complete the sentences.

1 Elina is **_Darren's_** sister.
2 His _____ name is Elizabeth.
3 'What's _____ job?' 'He's a chef.'
4 'Where's _____ apartment?' 'It's in Sydney.'

Talking about you

3 Write the names of people in your family.

Elvan   Maria

Ask and answer questions with a partner.

> Who's Elvan? — He's my brother/father.

> Who's Maria? — She's my mother/daughter.

> How old is he/she? — He's/She's ...

> What's his/her job? — He's/She's a ...

my/your/his ...

4 Complete the sentences with *my, your, his, ...* .

~~my~~   your   his   her   our   their (x2)

1 'What's your name?'
   '**_My_** name's Annie.'
2 'What are _____ names?'
   'Our names are Emma and Vince.'
3 Jean-Paul and André are students. _____ school is in Paris.
4 'My sister's married.'
   'What's _____ husband's name?
5 'My brother's office is in New York.'
   'Really? What's _____ job?'
6 We're in _____ English class.
7 'Mum and Dad are in Rome.'
   'What's the name of _____ hotel?'

🔊 **4.8** Listen and check.

> ▶ Go online to **watch** a video about Ethan Followwill and his family.

Grammar

Common verbs (1): *have/has, love, like, work*

1 Look at the photos. Who are the people?

2 🔊 **4.9** Listen and read about the family.

3 Are the sentences true (✓) or false (✗)?

1 ☒ The Beckhams' children are all boys.
   No, they aren't. The Beckhams have three boys and one girl.

2 ☐ David Beckham is a footballer and works for UNICEF.

3 ☐ David's wife, Victoria, is a fashion model.

4 ☐ Their daughter is a model for Burberry.

5 ☐ Brooklyn sometimes works in a shop.

6 ☐ Louise is David's sister.

7 ☐ They have houses in England and America.

8 ☐ They all like family time at home.

● **GRAMMAR SPOT**

I You We They	like love work have	He She It	likes loves works has

➔ Grammar reference 4.3 ▶ p40

---

4 🔊 **4.10** Listen and complete the sentences. Practise them.

1 We _____ three sons.

2 _____ children all _____ football.

3 _____ sister _____ a fashion boutique.

4 _____ son _____ there on Saturdays.

5 We _____ _____ house in France.

6 _____ parents _____ hard.

Talking about you

5 Talk about your family. Tell the class.

> I have two brothers.

> We have a small house in the centre of town.

Football star, DAVID BECKHAM, and his family

The Beckhams are a very famous family. David Beckham is a world famous footballer and his wife, Victoria, has a fashion business. They **have** four children: three sons – Brooklyn, Romeo and Cruz, and a daughter, Harper. Both football and fashion are important for the family – *all* the children **love** football, even little Harper. Victoria's sister, Louise, **has** a fashion boutique and Brooklyn works there on Saturdays. Romeo is a fashion model for *Burberry*. They're a rich family – they have four houses: in London, California, Dubai and the South of France, but they are a 'normal' family, too – they **like** family time at home. The parents work hard – they have a charity for young people, *The Victoria and David Beckham Charitable Trust*, and David **works** for UNICEF.

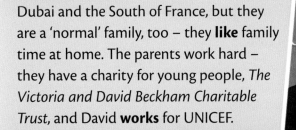

Practice

Common verbs

1 Complete the sentences. Use *is/are* or *have/has*.

1 I _**have**_ two sisters and a brother.
2 My sisters _____ both very pretty.
3 My little sister, Rosie, _____ only ten.
4 Our house _____ a big garden.
5 Our parents both _____ jobs in town.
6 My school _____ 20 classrooms.
7 I _____ a lot of friends.
8 We _____ all very happy at school.

2 Talk about your school/college.

> Our college is big.   We have twelve students in our class.
>
> I have English classes in the morning.

3 Complete the sentences with the verb in the correct form.

1 My mum's a head teacher. She _**loves**_ her job. (*love*)
2 My dad _____ in a very big hotel. (*work*)
3 It _____ 60 bedrooms and a swimming pool. (*have*)
4 My brother, Edward, _____ playing video games a lot. (*like*)
5 Our dog's called Rex. We all _____ him very much. (*love*)
6 Rex _____ our garden. (*love*)

🔊 **4.11** Listen and check.

Check it

4 Tick (✔) the correct sentence.

1 ✔ What's your daughter's name?
　　☐ What's your daughter name?
2 ☐ What's he's job?
　　☐ What's his job?
3 ☐ He has two brothers.
　　☐ He have two brothers.
4 ☐ Her brother, Dan, loves football.
　　☐ Her brother, Dan, love football.
5 ☐ Their parents have a house in town.
　　☐ They're parents has a house in town.
6 ☐ We likes our English lessons.
　　☐ We like our English lessons.
7 ☐ Our teacher work hard.
　　☐ Our teachers work hard.

☐→ Go online for more **grammar** practice

Reading and writing
My e-pal

1 🔊 **4.12** Listen and read about Melisa. What's her job?

2 Match the photos with a part of the text. Who are the people in the photos?

3 Tick (✔) the correct information.

1 Lisa is …
　☐ a student.　　　✔ a receptionist.
　☐ a nurse.　　　☐ married.
　✔ funny.　　　✔ 22.

2 Lisa has …
　☐ two sisters.　　☐ a boyfriend.
　☐ two brothers.　☐ a lot of fun.

3 Mehmet is …
　☐ Lisa's brother.　☐ a student.
　☐ Lisa's boyfriend.　☐ a waiter.
　☐ Lisa's father.

4 Arif is …
　☐ Lisa's boyfriend.　☐ a tennis fan.
　☐ Lisa's brother.　☐ at university.

5 Lisa's parents have …
　☐ an apartment.　☐ two sons.
　☐ a house.　　☐ two children.

6 Lisa likes …
　☐ football.　　☐ ballet.
　☐ tennis.　　　☐ Turkish dancing.
　☐ Marsel llhan.

4 🔊 **4.13** Listen to the people. Who are they?

1 _**Lisa**_　3 _____　5 _____　7 _____
2 _____　4 _____　6 _____　8 _____

Writing

5 Write about a friend of yours – his/her family, job, interests. Read it to your partner.

My friend's name is …　She/He has …
Her/His brother …　She/He likes …
She's/He's …

☐→ Go online for more **writing** practice

My e-pal Melisa

a My e-pal's name is Melisa – Lisa for short, and she's from Turkey. She's very funny and I like her emails; they're always very interesting. Lisa is 22 and she's a receptionist at the Hotel Amira in Istanbul. She loves her job. She likes meeting interesting people from around the world.

b She has a great boyfriend from Cyprus. He has a job at the hotel, too. His name is Mehmet and he's a waiter in the hotel bar.

c Lisa is from Adana in the south of Turkey. Her parents have a house near the city centre. Her father is Turkish and he works at one of Adana's airports. Her mother is English and is a businesswoman.

d She has two brothers. Their names are Arif and Basir. Arif is 17 and Basir is 14. They're both still at school.

e Lisa has a lot of interests, but her favourite hobby is dancing. She loves traditional Turkish dancing and dances in a lot of competitions. She also likes tennis. She and her brother, Arif, are big fans of Marsel Ilhan.

I learn a lot about Turkey from Lisa and it's really interesting. We have fun emailing and texting.

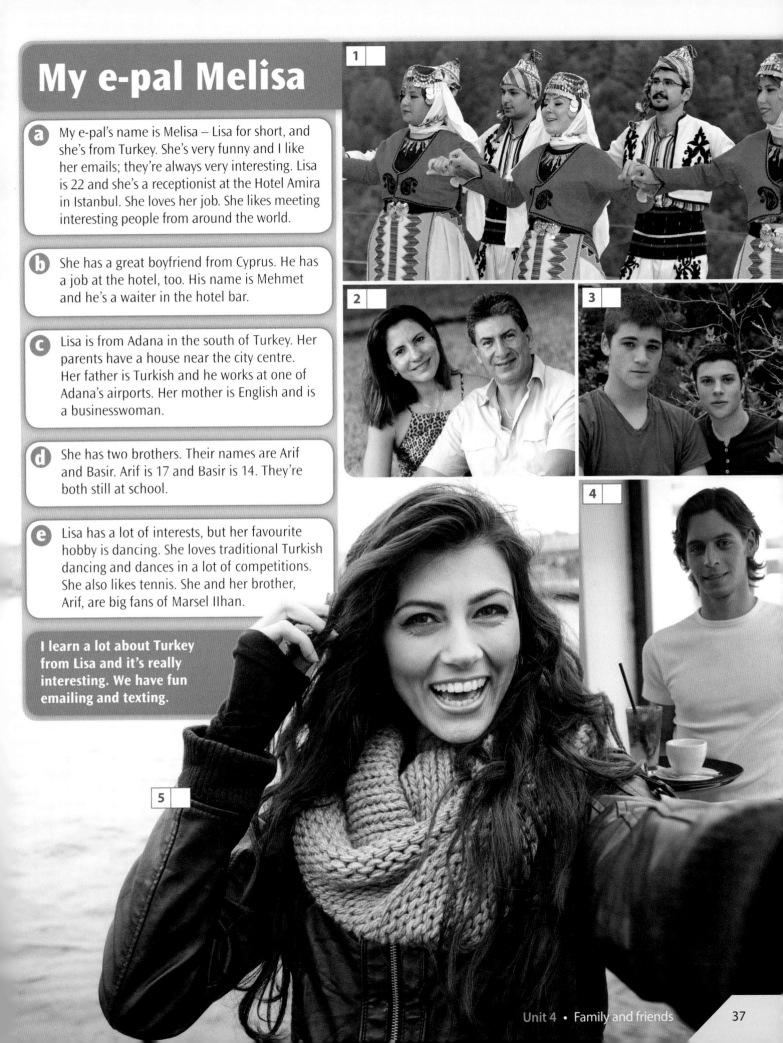

1

2

3

4

5

Vocabulary and speaking
The alphabet

Aa Bb Cc Dd Ee Ff
Gg Hh Ii Jj Kk Ll Mm
Nn Oo Pp Qq Rr Ss Tt
Uu Vv Ww Xx Yy Zz

1 ◀)) 4.14 Listen to the letters of the alphabet. Practise them.

2 ◀)) 4.15 Listen and practise the groups of letters.

/eɪ/ a h j k	/əʊ/ o
/iː/ b c d e g p t v	/uː/ q u w
/e/ f l m n s x z	/ɑː/ r
/aɪ/ i y	

How do you spell …?

3 ◀)) 4.16 Listen to people spell their first names and their surname. Write the names.

1 *BECKY* *McCAUL*
2 _____ _____
3 _____ _____
4 _____ _____
5 _____ _____

4 Practise spelling your name with a partner.

> How do you spell your first name? H-E-L-E-N-A

> How do you spell your surname? B-A-S-C-O

5 Work with a partner. Ask and answer the question *How do you spell …?*

> How do you spell 'people'? P-E-O-P-L-E

6 Put the letters in the correct order. What's the country?

K T R U Y E	T*urkey*_____
X C M I O E	M_____
U S R A A I T L A	A_____
N C I H A	C_____
L E N A R I D	I_____
P I A N S	S_____
Y I L A T	I_____

7 Read the letters aloud. What are they?

PC   WWW   TV
ID   UAE   UK   US
BBC   EU   VIP

◀)) 4.17 Listen and check.

Everyday English
On the phone

1 Look at the two business cards. What businesses are they for?

2 🔊 4.18 Listen and complete Conversation 1.

3 🔊 4.18 Listen again and check. Practise the conversation with your partner.

4 🔊 4.19 Listen and complete Conversation 2.

5 🔊 4.19 Listen again and check. Answer the questions.
1 What's the name of the hotel?
2 What does Ian want?
3 Is there a room free?
4 What's Ian's email address?

Email addresses

6 Notice how we say email addresses.

@	at	**com**	/kɒm/
.	dot	**co**	/kəʊ/
		uk	/ˌjuː ˈkeɪ/ (United Kingdom)
		ca	/ˌsiː ˈeɪ/ (Canada)

7 🔊 4.20 Listen and complete the email addresses.

> **btinternet**   **toronto**
> **wanadoo**   hotmail   **yahoo**

1 pam_____@btinternet_____
2 harrylime_____
3 paul_____wanadoo_____
4 glennamiles_____

What's your email address? Tell a partner.

Talking about you

8 Work with your partner. Practise the conversations with information about you.

🔗 Go online for more **speaking** practice

Operator Good ¹_____. Perez Taxis.

Anita Hello. Can I book a taxi for 11.15 this morning, please?

O Certainly. What's ²_____ name?

A It's Anita Jarvis.

O How do you ³_____ your ⁴_____?

A J-A-R-V-I-S.

O Thank you. What's your ⁵_____?

A 24 Avenida Balboa.

O And ⁶_____ do you want to go?

A Centro Santa Fe.

O And your phone number, please?

A ⁷_____

O OK! Your taxi is booked for 11.15.

A Thank you very ⁸_____.

PEREZ TAXIS
Emiliano Zapata Street
Polanco
06767 Mexico

Tel: 09-967-454-08
Email: Perez.taxis@mailchimp.com

Conversation 2

Lisa Good ¹_____. The Hotel Amira.

Ian Hello. Do you have a Family Deluxe room from 12–14 July?

Lisa Let me check. Yes, we ²_____ one family room left.

Ian Excellent. Can we have that, please?

Lisa Of course. And your name is?

Ian Ian McCaul.

Lisa McCaul … Sorry. How do you ³_____ your surname?

Ian M-C-C-A-U-L.

Lisa Thank you. And can I have ⁴_____ email address, please?

Ian It's ianmccaul@yippee.co.uk.

Lisa Thank you. I'll send you an email confirmation. Have a ⁵_____ day.

Ian Thank you.

Hotel Amira
Istanbul

Mustafa Paşa Sk. No:43, 34122, Turkey
Tel: +90 212 516 1640
www.hotelamira.com
Email: info@hotelamiro.com

Grammar reference

→ 4.1 Possessive adjectives

This is	my your his her our their	family. school. office.

→ 4.2 Possessive 's

's shows possession.

This is John. This is his bike.	→	This is John's bike.
This is Marie. This is her car.	→	This is Marie's car.
Kelly and Tim are married. This is their son.	→	This is Kelly and Tim's son.

his house	→	Noel's house
her name	→	your wife's name
their daughter	→	Pam and Bob's daughter

❶ 's is also the short form of *is*.

he's	=	he **is**
she's	=	she **is**
it's	=	it **is**
Who's	=	Who **is**

→ 4.3 Common verbs

I You We They	like love	football.
	work	in an office.
He She It	like**s** love**s**	football.
	work**s**	in an office.

Have is an irregular verb.

I You We They	**have**	a good job. a laptop.
He She It	**has**	

Wordlist

adj = adjective	*n* = noun	*prep* = preposition
adv = adverb	*phr* = phrase	*pron* = pronoun
conj = conjunction	*pl* = plural	*v* = verb

airport   *n*   /'eəpɔːt/   _____
a lot of   /ə 'lɒt əv/   _____
apartment   *n*   /ə'pɑːtmənt/   _____
at home   *adv*   /ət 'həʊm/   _____
boy   *n*   /bɔɪ/   _____
boyfriend   *n*   /'bɔɪfrend/   _____
business card   *n*   /'bɪznəs ˌkɑːd/   _____
businesswoman   *n*   /'bɪznəswʊmən/   _____
charity   *n*   /'tʃærəti/   _____
chef   *n*   /ʃef/   _____
children   *n pl*   /'tʃɪldrən/   _____
class   *n*   /klɑːs/   _____
classroom   *n*   /'klɑːsruːm/   _____
college   *n*   /'kɒlɪdʒ/   _____
competition   *n*   /ˌkɒmpə'tɪʃn/   _____
dance   *v*   /dɑːns/   _____
dancing   *n*   /'dɑːnsɪŋ/   _____
dog   *n*   /dɒg/   _____
e-pal   *n*   /'iː pæl/   _____
famous   *adj*   /'feɪməs/   _____
fan   *n*   /fæn/   _____
fashion   *n*   /'fæʃn/   _____
friend   *n*   /frend/   _____
funny   *adj*   /'fʌni/   _____
hard   *adv*   /hɑːd/   _____
have   *v*   /hæv/   _____
have fun   *phr*   /hæv 'fʌn/   _____
head teacher   *n*   /ˌhed 'tiːtʃə(r)/   _____
important   *adj*   /ɪm'pɔːtnt/   _____
interest   *n*   /'ɪntrəst/   _____
like   *v*   /laɪk/   _____
love   *v*   /lʌv/   _____
model   *n*   /'mɒdl/   _____
Northern Ireland   *n*   /ˌnɔːðən 'aɪələnd/   _____
people   *n pl*   /'piːpl/   _____
rich   *adj*   /rɪtʃ/   _____
school   *n*   /skuːl/   _____
schoolgirl   *n*   /'skuːlgɜːl/   _____
shop   *n*   /ʃɒp/   _____
spell   *v*   /spel/   _____
tennis   *n*   /'tenɪs/   _____
text   *v*   /tekst/   _____
traditional   *adj*   /trə'dɪʃənl/   _____
Turkish   *adj*   /'tɜːkɪʃ/   _____
university   *n*   /ˌjuːnɪ'vɜːsəti/   _____
work   *v*   /wɜːk/   _____
young   *adj*   /jʌŋ/   _____   -

The family
brother   *n*   /'brʌðə(r)/   _____
daughter   *n*   /'dɔːtə(r)/   _____
father   *n*   /'fɑːðə(r)/   _____
husband   *n*   /'hʌzbənd/   _____
mother   *n*   /'mʌðə(r)/   _____
parents   *n pl*   /'peərənts/   _____
sister   *n*   /'sɪstə(r)/   _____
son   *n*   /sʌn/   _____
wife   *n*   /waɪf/   _____

Things I like! 5

- Grammar **Present Simple – *I/you/we/they***
- Vocabulary **Languages and nationalities; Adjective + noun (1)**
- Everyday English **Numbers and prices**
- Reading **Alek Brosko from Warsaw**
- Listening **Party time**

?

1 Write the names of two countries, two foods, two drinks and two sports you like.

2 Work with a partner. Compare your lists.

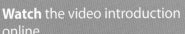 **Watch** the video introduction online

 Use your **Workbook** for self study

 Go online for more practice and to *Check your Progress*

Likes and dislikes

1 Match the words and pictures.

| golf coffee chicken strawberries tea tennis Italian food crisps |
| baseball milkshake tomatoes wine beer chocolate water swimming |

SPORTS

1 golf
2
3
4

FOOD

5
6
7

8
9
10

DRINKS

11
12
13

14
15
16

🔊 **5.1** Listen and repeat.

2 Tick (✓) the things you like. ☺   Cross (✗) the things you don't like. ☹

Grammar
Present Simple positive

1 🔊 **5.2** Listen and repeat.

I like chocolate.

I like baseball.

2 Say three things you like from pictures 1–16.

> I like tea, strawberries and swimming.

🔗 **Go online** for more **vocabulary** practice

Present Simple negative

3 **5.3** Listen and repeat.

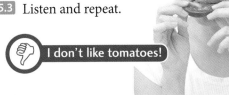

> 👎 I don't like tomatoes!

> 👎 I don't like football!

4 Say three things you don't like from pictures 1–16 on page 42.

> I don't like beer, tomatoes or baseball.

● GRAMMAR SPOT

Positive	I **like** chocolate.	
Negative	I **don't like** tomatoes.	**don't** = do not

5 **5.4** Listen to Dexter. Complete the text.

Dexter

Sports

'I like ¹ *sports* a lot. I like
² _____ and ³_____,
and I love ⁴_____ but I don't
like golf very much.'

Food and drink

'I like ⁵ *ice cream* and ⁶_____. And I like
⁷_____ food a lot. But I don't like ⁸_____
and I really don't like ⁹_____. I really love
¹⁰_____ _____!'

Questions – I/you/we/they

6 **5.5** Listen and repeat.

Do you **like** golf?	**Yes**, I **do**.	❓
Do you **like** tennis?	**No**, I **don't**.	

7 Work with a partner. Ask and answer about sports, food and drinks.

> Do you like golf?
> Yes, I do.

> Do you like baseball?
> No, I don't, but I like tennis.

8 **5.6** Dexter has a little sister, Daisy. Listen to them. What do they like? (✓) What don't they like? (✗) What do they say? Write the adjectives.

disgusting   boring
delicious   ~~great~~
fantastic
   horrible
cool   exciting

		Daisy	Dexter	
1	ice cream	✓	✓	*great*
2	chocolate	___	___	_____
3	milkshake	___	___	_____
4	tomatoes	___	___	_____	_____
5	tennis	___	___	_____
6	baseball	___	___	_____	_____

9 Talk about Dexter and Daisy with a partner. What do they like?

> They like ice cream and ….

● GRAMMAR SPOT

Positive	I/You/We/They **like** chocolate.
Negative	I/You/We/They **don't like** golf.
Questions	What **do** you/they **like**?
	Do you/they **like** ….?
Short answers	**Yes**, I/we/they **do**.
	No, I/we/they **don't**.

> ▶ Go online to **watch** a video about an international food market.

Practice

Alek's life

1 Look at the photos and the title. Where is Alek from? What's his job? What are his interests?

🔊 5.7 Listen and read about Alex Brosko. Check your answers.

Alek Brosko
FROM
Warsaw

"Hi! My name's Alek Brosko. I come from Warsaw in Poland, but now I live and work in Bristol. I live with my wife, Bella and my six-year-old son, Danek. We have an apartment near the centre. I have my own car wash business, but I'm also a ballroom dancer – my wife is too. We both love ballroom dancing!

I'm Polish and my wife is Italian, so in our home we speak three languages, Polish, Italian and English. We usually speak English because I don't speak Italian very well! We eat a lot of Italian food and I like French wine and... I love an English cup of tea. I don't like beer, but all my English friends love it! I don't like sports very much, but I love football – Danek and I are big Bristol Rovers fans. I want to be a famous dancer one day, with my wife, of course!"

2 🔊 **5.8** Listen to the conversation with Alek. Complete his answers.

1 Where do you come from?
I _come_ from Poland, from Warsaw.

2 Do you live in London?
No, I _don't_ . I _____ and _____ in Bristol.

3 Do you like Bristol?
Yes, I _____ . I _____ it a lot. It's an _____ city.

4 Do you live with friends?
No, I _____ . I _____ with my wife and son.

5 What languages do you speak at home?
We usually _____ English. I _____ speak Italian very well.

6 Do you drink English beer?
No, I _____ . I _____ like it. But I _____ English tea.

7 Where do you work?
In the city centre. I _____ my own car wash business.

8 Do you like your job?
Yes, I _____ , but my wife and I want to be professional ballroom _____ one day.

🔊 **5.8** Listen again and check. Practise the questions.

3 Ask and answer the questions with a partner. Give *true* answers about *you*.

4 Match a verb in **A** with a line in **B**.

A	B
have	to have a big house
live	Italian food
work	tennis
come	in an apartment
eat	English and French
drink	coffee
play	in an office
speak	two children
want	from Turkey

● **GRAMMAR SPOT**

Positive	I/You/We/They **live** in a big house.
Negative	I/You/We/They **don't play** baseball.
Questions	**Do** you/they **speak** Polish?
	Where **do** you/they **come** from?

➔ Grammar reference 5.1 ▶ p50

Listening and speaking

5 🔊 **5.9** Listen to four conversations. Where is Alek? Who says these lines?

1 a *Bye, Daddy. Have a good day, too.*
  b *Thanks, honey! See you later!*

2 a *What do I get for £10?*
  b *We do a good job!*

3 a *Are you all ready?*
  b *Oops! Sorry!*

4 a *It's cold today.*
  b *A great goal!*

Look at audioscript 5.9 on page 142. Practise the conversations.

Talking about you

6 Work with a partner. Complete the questions, then ask and answer them about *you*.

1 Where _____ you come from?
2 Do you _____ in a house or an apartment?
3 Where _____ you work?
4 _____ you like your work?
5 How many languages _____ you _____ ?
6 Do you _____ Italian food?
7 What sports _____ you _____ ?
8 _____ you _____ to have a big house?

Check it

7 Tick (✓) the correct answer.

1 ☐ Live you in Warsaw?
  ✓ Do you live in Warsaw?

2 ☐ Where do you come from?
  ☐ Where you come from?

3 ☐ Are you speak Spanish?
  ☐ Do you speak Spanish?

4 ☐ I don't speak Turkish.
  ☐ I not speak Turkish.

5 ☐ 'Do you like football?' 'Yes, I like.'
  ☐ 'Do you like football?' 'Yes, I do.'

6 ☐ 'Do you have a big house?' 'No, I don't.'
  ☐ 'Do you have a big house?' 'No, I don't have.'

🔗 **Go online** for more **grammar** practice

Vocabulary
Languages and nationalities

1 Match the countries and nationalities.

England	American
Turkey	Italian
Mexico	Scottish
Italy	Mexican
Spain	Polish
Ireland	Chinese
Scotland	Swiss
China	German
Germany	English
Switzerland	Brazilian
Brazil	Irish
the United States	Turkish
Poland	Spanish

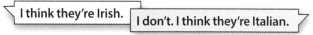 **5.10** Listen and repeat.

2 Look at the photos. What nationality are the people?

> I think they're Irish.
> I don't. I think they're Italian.

3 Match the countries with the languages they speak.

> In Switzerland they speak French and German.

Switzerland	English
the United States	French
Brazil	German
Mexico	Portuguese
Ireland	Arabic
Egypt	Japanese
Canada	Turkish
Japan	Spanish
Turkey	Gaelic

 **5.11** Listen and check.

4 Ask and answer questions with a partner.

> What language do they speak in Ireland?
> English and Gaelic.

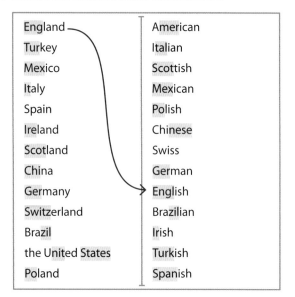

Adjective + noun (1)

5 What are they? Where are they from?

1 It's _Turkish_ coffee.

2 It's _____ food.

3 They're _____ jeans.

4 It's _____ bread.

5 It's _____ whisky.

6 It's _____ beer.

7 It's a _____ car.

8 It's an _____ dictionary.

9 They're _____ shoes.

🔊 **5.12** Listen and check. Practise the sentences.

Talking about you

6 Talk about you. Use the verbs *have*, *eat*, and *drink*.

I drink Scottish whisky. I don't drink English beer.

7 Ask and answer questions with a partner.

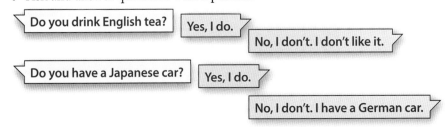

Do you drink English tea?　Yes, I do.

No, I don't. I don't like it.

Do you have a Japanese car?　Yes, I do.

No, I don't. I have a German car.

● **GRAMMAR SPOT**

1 Adjectives come before the noun.

a **Japanese** car

Scottish whisky NOT ~~whisky Scottish~~

2 We don't add **-s** to the adjective.

Italian shoes NOT Italian~~s~~ shoes

➔ Grammar reference 5.2 ⟩ **p50**

📤 Go online for more **vocabulary** practice

Listening and speaking
Party time

1 🔊 5.13 Daniel and Tam meet at a party in London. Look at the photo and listen to their conversation. Do they know each other well or not very well?

2 🔊 5.13 Listen again. Tick (✓) the lines Daniel says.

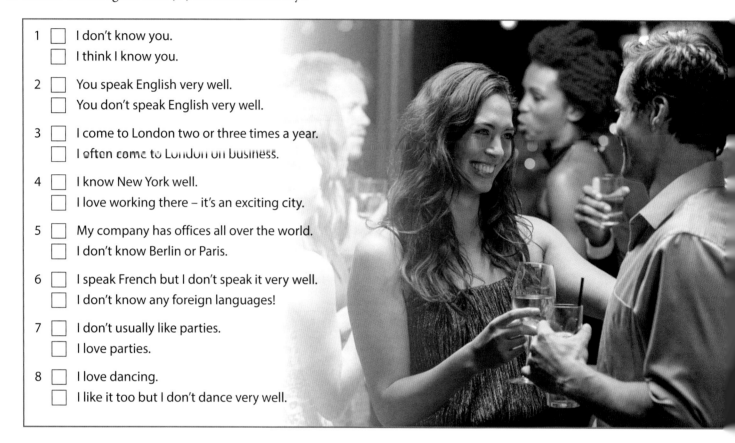

1 ☐ I don't know you.
  ☐ I think I know you.

2 ☐ You speak English very well.
  ☐ You don't speak English very well.

3 ☐ I come to London two or three times a year.
  ☐ I often come to London on business.

4 ☐ I know New York well.
  ☐ I love working there – it's an exciting city.

5 ☐ My company has offices all over the world.
  ☐ I don't know Berlin or Paris.

6 ☐ I speak French but I don't speak it very well.
  ☐ I don't know any foreign languages!

7 ☐ I don't usually like parties.
  ☐ I love parties.

8 ☐ I love dancing.
  ☐ I like it too but I don't dance very well.

Look at audioscript 5.13 on page 142. Practise the conversation with a partner.

Roleplay

3 Work with a partner. You meet at a party.
Think of some questions to ask.

- Hello! What's …?
- Where … from?
- What's … job?
- Where … work?
- How many languages … speak?
- Who … you know at the party?
- … like the music?
- What music … you like?
- … like dancing?

4 Think of a new identity. Make notes to answer the questions in exercise 4.

5 Stand up. Find out about your new classmates!

Everyday English
How much is it?

1 Count from 1–30 round the class.

2 🔊 5.14 Listen and repeat.

10 ten   **20** twenty

30 thirty   **40** forty

50 fifty   **60** sixty

70 seventy   **80** eighty

90 ninety   **100** one hundred

Count to 100 in tens round the class.

3 Work with a partner.

Student A
Write some numbers. Say them to your partner.

> thirty-seven
> sixty-five
> forty-two

Student B
Write the numbers you hear.
37   65 …

4 🔊 5.15 Read and listen to the prices. Practise them.

30p thirty p /piː/   **50p** fifty p

75p seventy-five p   **£1** one pound

£20 twenty pounds   **£75** seventy-five pounds

£1.60 one pound sixty

£3.45 three pounds forty-five

£22.80 twenty-two pounds eighty

5 Say the prices.

60p	**97p**	**£17**	**£70**
£25	**£1.50**	**£3.99**	**£16.80**
£46.99	**€20**	**€50**	**$100**

🔊 5.16 Listen and check.

6 🔊 5.17 Listen and tick (✓) the prices you hear.

1 £2.99 ☐   £2.90 ☐   **2** 60p ☐   70p ☐

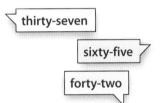

3 £65 ☐   £75 ☐   **4** £7.50 ☐   £7.15 ☐

5 £200 ☐   £300 ☐   **6** €3.80 ☐   €3.20 ☐

7 €4.50 ☐   €4.60 ☐   **8** $75.99 ☐ $75.90 ☐

7 Ask and answer questions about the photos in exercise 6 with a partner.

> How much is the cheese sandwich?   £2.99

📤 Go online for more **speaking** practice

Grammar reference

→ 5.1 Present Simple: *I/you/we/they*

Positive

I You We They	**like** coffee. **play** tennis. **live** in London. **speak** two languages. **have** a good job.

Negative

I You We They	**don't**	**like** tennis. **speak** French. **work** in a restaurant.

Questions with question words

Where		you **live**?
What sports	**do**	we **like**?
How many languages		they **speak**?

Yes/No questions and short answers

Do you **like** football?	Yes, I **do**. No, I **don't**.
Do they **speak** English?	Yes, they **do**. No, they **don't**.

❶ *Do you like tea?* Yes, I do. NOT ~~Yes, I like.~~

→ 5.2 Adjective + noun (1)

Adjectives always come before the noun.

*an **English** dictionary*		~~*a dictionary English*~~
*a **Japanese** car*	NOT	~~*a car Japanese*~~
*a **beautiful** girl*		~~*a girl beautiful*~~

❶ ***Italian** shoes* NOT ~~Italians shoes~~

Wordlist

adj = adjective	*n* = noun	*prep* = preposition
adv = adverb	*phr v* = phrasal verb	*pron* = pronoun
conj = conjunction	*pl* = plural	*v* = verb

Arabic   *n* /'ærəbɪk/ _____
baseball   *n* /'beɪsbɔːl/ _____
beer   *n* /bɪə(r)/ _____
boring   *adj* /'bɔːrɪŋ/ _____
bread *n* /bred/ _____
cheese   *n* /tʃiːz/ _____
chocolate   *n* /'tʃɒklət/ _____
come from   *phr v* /'kʌm frɒm/ _____
cool   *adj* /kuːl/ _____
crisps   *n pl* /krɪsps/ _____
delicious   *adj* /dɪ'lɪʃəs/ _____
dictionary   *n* /'dɪkʃənri/ _____
disgusting   *adj* /dɪs'ɡʌstɪŋ/ _____
drink   *n, v* /drɪŋk/ _____
eat   *v* /iːt/ _____
exciting   *adj* /ɪk'saɪtɪŋ/ _____
food   *n* /fuːd/ _____
golf   *n* /ɡɒlf/ _____
horrible   *adj* /'hɒrəbl/ _____
How much?   /,haʊ 'mʌtʃ/ _____
ice cream   *n* /'aɪskriːm/ _____
jeans   *n pl* /dʒiːnz/ _____
language   *n* /'læŋɡwɪdʒ/ _____
live   *v* /lɪv/ _____
milkshake   *n* /'mɪlkʃeɪk/ _____
nationality   *n* /,næʃə'næləti/ _____
play   *v* /pleɪ/ _____
pound   *n* /paʊnd/ _____
shoes   *n pl* /ʃuːz/ _____
speak   *v* /spiːk/ _____
strawberries   *n pl* /'strɔːbəriz/ _____
swimming   *n* /'swɪmɪŋ/ _____
tomatoes   *n pl* /tə'mɑːtəʊz/ _____
wine   *n* /waɪn/ _____
whisky   *n* /'wɪski/ _____

Nationalities
American   *adj* /ə'merɪkən/ _____
Brazilian   *adj* /brə'zɪliən/ _____
Chinese   *adj* /tʃaɪ'niːz/ _____
French   *adj* /frentʃ/ _____
German   *adj* /'dʒɜːmən/ _____
Irish   *adj* /'aɪrɪʃ/ _____
Italian   *adj* /ɪ'tæliən/ _____
Japanese   *adj* /,dʒæpə'niːz/ _____
Mexican   *adj* /'meksɪkən/ _____
Polish   *adj* /'pəʊlɪʃ/ _____
Portuguese   *adj* /,pɔːtʃu'ɡiːz/ _____
Scottish   *adj* /'skɒtɪʃ/ _____
Spanish   *adj* /'spænɪʃ/ _____
Swiss   *adj* /swɪs/ _____

Numbers 40–100
forty   /'fɔːti/ _____
fifty   /'fɪfti/ _____
sixty   /'sɪksti/ _____
seventy   /'sevnti/ _____
eighty   /'eɪti/ _____
ninety   /'naɪnti/ _____
one hundred   /,wʌn 'hʌndrəd/ _____

Every day **6**

- Grammar **Present Simple – *I/you/he/she; always/sometimes/never***
- Vocabulary **The time; Words that go together**
- Everyday English **Days of the week; *in/on/at***

1 Tick the things you do every day.
- [ ] drink coffee
- [ ] eat cake
- [ ] play football
- [ ] speak English
- [ ] work

2 Work with a partner. Compare your lists.

What time is it?

1 🔊 **6.1** Listen and repeat. Write the times.

1 It's nine o'clock. | **2** It's nine thirty. | **3** It's nine forty-five. | **4** It's ten o'clock. | **5** It's ten fifteen.

    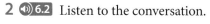

2:00 | 2:30 | 2:45 | 3:00 | 3:15

6 | **7** | **8** | **9** | **10**

2 🔊 **6.2** Listen to the conversation.

A What time is it, please?
B It's nine o'clock.
A Thank you very much.

3 Work with a partner. Ask and answer questions about the times on this page.

4 What time is it now?

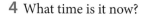

3

4

12:30

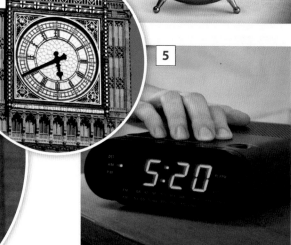

1

2

5

5:20

6

8:15

📲 Go online for more **vocabulary** practice

52   Unit 6 • Every day

Grammar
Present Simple – *I/you*

1 🔊 **6.3** Felipe is a shop assistant at a big supermarket. Listen to Felipe talking about his working day. Circle the times.

1 I get up at *6.00 / 6.45*.

2 I have breakfast at *6.30 / 7.00*.

3 I go to work at *7.15 / 7.30*.

4 I have lunch at *12.00 / 12.15*.

5 I leave work at *4.30 / 4.45*.

6 I get home at *5.00 / 5.15*.

7 I go to bed at *10.30 / 10.45*.

🔊 **6.3** Listen again. Practise the sentences.

Talking about you

2 Work with a partner. Talk about your day.
I get up at 7.30. I have breakfast at …

3 🔊 **6.4** Listen and repeat the questions.

What time **do** you **get up**?
What time **do** you **have** breakfast?

4 Work with a partner. Ask and answer questions about your day.

What time do you get up?
I get up at 7.15.

Present Simple – *he/she;*
always/sometimes/never

Anna's day

1 Read about Anna McMann and look at the photos. Are her days busy?

2 Read the sentences about Anna's day. Write the times.

1 She <u>gets up</u> at *6 o'clock* and she <u>has</u> a shower.
2 She has breakfast at _____ .
3 She leaves home at _____ and she cycles to work.
4 She has lunch (a wrap and salad) at _____ .
5 She always works late. She leaves the hospital at _____ .
6 She sometimes buys a Chinese takeaway and eats it at home with her brother, Toby. She has her dinner at _____ .
7 She never goes out in the week. She works for her exams until _____ .
8 She always goes to bed at _____ and watches TV or reads a book.

🔊 6.5 Listen and check.

● GRAMMAR SPOT

1 <u>Underline</u> the verbs in sentences 1–8. What's the last letter?

   cycles   *works*

   🔊 6.6 Listen to the verbs and repeat.

2 Look at the adverbs.

   | 100% —— 50% —— 0% |

   | always   sometimes   never |

   🔊 6.7 Listen to the sentences and repeat.

3 Find *always*, *sometimes* and *never* in exercise 2.

➔ Grammar reference 6.1–6.3 ▶ p60

Pronunciation

3 🔊 6.8 Listen to the pronunciation of *-s* at the end of the verbs. Practise the verbs.

/s/	/z/		/ɪz/
get**s** up	read**s**	leave**s**	watche**s**
work**s**	cycle**s**	buy**s**	
eat**s**	goe**s**	doe**s**	

A day in the life of Anna

Anna lives in London. She's 29 and a junior doctor at a big hospital in the centre of London. The hospital is always busy. This is a typical day.

1
6.00 AM

2
6.30 AM

3
7.00 AM

4
12.30 PM

5
7.45 PM

6

8.15 PM

7

10.30 PM

8

10.45 PM

Questions and negatives

4 Read the questions. Complete the answers.

> 1 What time **does** she **get up**?
>   She _____ at 6.00.
>
> 2 When **does** she **go** to bed?
>   She _____ to bed at 10.45.
>
> 3 **Does** she **go** to work by car?
>   _____, she **doesn't**.
>
> 4 **Does** she **go** to work by bike?
>   _____, she **does**.
>
> 5 **Does** she **have** lunch at home?
>   _____, she **doesn't**.
>
> 6 **Does** she **work** for her exams in the evening?
>   _____, she **does**.

◄))) 6.9 Listen and check. Practise the questions and answers.

● GRAMMAR SPOT

Positive	She **gets up** at 6.00. She **has** breakfast at 6.30.	
Negative	She **doesn't have** lunch at home. She **doesn't go** to work by car.	**doesn't** = does not
Questions	What time **does** she **get up**? **Does** she **work** late? Yes, she **does**. / No, she **doesn't**.	

➔ Grammar reference 6.4 ▶ p60

5 Work with a partner. Ask and answer the questions about Anna's day.

1 When / leave home?	4 Does / usually work late?
2 Does / go to work by bus?	5 Does / eat in a restaurant?
3 Where / have lunch?	6 What / do in the evening?

◄))) 6.10 Listen and check.

6 Make negative sentences about Anna.

1 live / New York **She doesn't live in New York.**	3 work in a school
	4 visit friends in the week
2 drive / work	5 go to bed late

7 Complete the chart in the Present Simple.

	Positive	Negative	Question
I	*work*		*Do I work?*
You			
He/She	*works*		*Does he/she work?*
We		*don't work*	
They			

▶ **Go online** to **watch** a video about Sara's day.

Practice

Toby's day

1 Anna has a flatmate – Toby, her brother. His day is very different to Anna's. Look at the photos. What does he do?

2 Read and complete the text with the verbs.

| ~~shares~~ goes (x2) gets up eats loves walks |
| meets starts plays gets (x2) |

Toby McMann

The London dog walker fills his day with lots of walks, fresh air and fun!

Toby McMann is 31 and he's a dog walker and a student of music. He ¹ _shares_ a small flat in the centre of London with his sister, Anna.

He usually ² _____ at ten thirty in the morning. He has a big breakfast – tea, sausages, eggs and lots of toast – then he ³ _____ to work. He ⁴ _____ lots of dogs in the parks in London. He ⁵ _____ his job, it's fun!

Toby is a part-time student at the London College of Music. He ⁶ _____ classes at two fifteen in the afternoon.

He ⁷ _____ home at six o'clock in the evening and has a big dinner. He sometimes shares a Chinese takeaway with Anna when she ⁸ _____ home. He is always hungry in the evening because he never ⁹ _____ lunch.

He always ¹⁰ _____ his cello after dinner, but sometimes he ¹¹ _____ his friends. He usually ¹² _____ to bed very late, at one o'clock in the morning.

🔊 6.11 Listen and check.

3 Are these sentences about Toby or Anna? Write *He* or *She*.

1 _She_'s a doctor.
2 ___'s a student.
3 ___ gets up very early.
4 ___ cycles to work.
5 ___ walks a lot every day.
6 ___ doesn't have lunch.
7 ___ eats at work.
8 ___ sometimes goes out in the evening.

Listening

4 🔊 **6.12** Listen and complete the conversation between Anna and Toby.

Toby Evening, Anna. You look tired.
Anna I'm ¹ _fine_ , thanks. Just busy as usual.
Toby You're ² _____ busy. You work too hard!
Anna I know, but I ³ _____ my work and I have exams soon.
Toby I love my work, ⁴ _____ , but I sometimes relax and see my friends!
Anna Relax! You play the cello every day!
Toby Yes, but I ⁵ _____ a drink with my friends at the weekend. You ⁶ _____ stop!
Anna That's not true. We ⁷ _____ share a Chinese takeaway! Oh, Toby. How's your friend Oliver?
Toby He's fine, thanks. He ⁸ _____ asks about you. I think he likes you!
Anna Oliver is OK. I like him and he's a friend of yours.
Toby Well, come and meet us at the pub. I can buy you a ⁹ _____ !
Anna Really? That is a good idea. What about next ¹⁰ _____ ?
Toby Yes, great! I often ¹¹ _____ Oliver on Saturday.
Anna Good! Then it's a date!

🔊 **6.12** Listen again and check. Practise the conversation with a partner.

Negatives and pronunciation

5 Correct the sentences about Anna and Toby.

1 He's a doctor.
   He isn't a doctor. He's a student of music .

2 She gets up at ten thirty.
   _____ .

3 He's 29.
   _____ .

4 She goes to work by car.
   _____ .

5 She meets friends in the evening.
   _____ .

🔊 **6.13** Listen and check. Notice the sentence stress. Practise with a partner.

Talking about you

6 Work with a partner. Write the names of two people in your family, or friends. Ask and answer questions about them.

Maria — Who's she? — She's my sister.

Charles — Who's he? — He's my best friend.

- Who is …?
- How old is …?
- What's … job?
- Where does … live?
- What time does she/he …?
- Does she/he have …?

Check it

7 Complete the questions and answers with *do, don't, does* or *doesn't.*

1 '_____ you like pizza?'
   'Yes, I _____ .'

2 '_____ she work in London?'
   'Yes, she _____ .'

3 'Where _____ he work?'
   'In a hospital.'

4 '_____ you go to work by car?'
   'No, I _____ .'

5 '_____ she go to bed early?'
   'No, she _____ .'

6 '_____ they have a dog?'
   ' Yes, they _____ .'

7 '_____ he speak Spanish?'
   'No, he _____ .'

8 '_____ they live in Scotland?'
   'No, they _____ .'

🔗 Go online for more **grammar** practice

Vocabulary and speaking
Words that go together

1 Match a verb in **A** with a word or phrase in **B**.

A	B
get up	music
go	early
have	TV
watch	lunch
listen to	in a hospital
work	to bed late

A	B
stay	in restaurants
drink	the cello
eat	for friends
have	coffee
play	at home
cook	a shower

🔊 6.14 Listen and check.

2 🔊 6.15 Look at the questionnaire. Listen and repeat the questions.

{ **Lifestyle** *questionnaire* }

Do you …?

	always 100%	usually 75%	sometimes 25%	never 0%
1 get up early	☐	☐	☐	☐
2 have breakfast	☐	☐	☐	☐
3 walk to work or school	☐	☐	☐	☐
4 eat a lot of fruit	☐	☐	☐	☐
5 eat a lot of chocolate	☐	☐	☐	☐
6 play a sport	☐	☐	☐	☐
7 play computer games	☐	☐	☐	☐
8 drink fizzy drinks	☐	☐	☐	☐
9 drink a lot of water	☐	☐	☐	☐
10 eat fast food	☐	☐	☐	☐
11 go to bed late	☐	☐	☐	☐

3 Ask a partner the questions and complete the questionnaire. Tick (✓) the correct boxes.

Do you …?

Yes, usually.

Yes, sometimes.

No, never.

4 Tell the class about your partner.

Leo usually walks to work. He never eats chocolate.

🔗 Go online for more **vocabulary** practice

Everyday English

Days of the week

1 🔊 **6.16** Listen and write the days in the correct order on the calendar.

Wednesday ~~Monday~~ Friday Tuesday

Thursday Sunday Saturday

🔊 **6.16** Listen again and repeat.

2 Work with a partner. Ask and answer the questions.

1 What day is it today?
2 What day is it tomorrow?
3 What days do you go to work/school?
4 What days are the weekend?
5 What is your favourite day?
6 What day don't you like?

3 Write the correct prepositions in the boxes.

on   in   at

	nine o'clock
	ten thirty
	twelve fifteen
	the weekend
	Sunday
	Monday
	Saturday evening
	Thursday morning
	Friday afternoon
	the morning
	the afternoon
	the evening

4 Write the correct preposition. Then ask and answer the questions with your partner.

Do you have English lessons …?

1 *at* nine o'clock   4 ____ Monday morning
2 ____ Sunday   5 ____ the weekend
3 ____ the evening

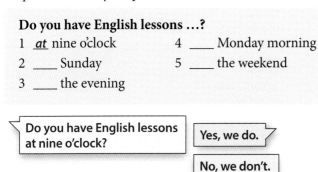

Do you have English lessons at nine o'clock?

Yes, we do.

No, we don't.

When do you have English lessons?

We have English lessons …

August

Monday	Doctor's 10:15	**15**
		16
	♡Visit mum♡	**17**
	'My Party!' ❀	**18**
		19
	Concert ☀	**20**
	SCHOOL PLAY, 7pm	**21**

Talking about you

5 Complete the questions. Ask and answer them with your partner.

Do you …?
• have a shower _____ the morning/evening
• get up early _____ Sunday morning
• go to work/school _____ Saturday
• eat in restaurants _____ the weekend
• watch TV _____ the evening
• stay at home _____ Saturday evening

↗ Go online for more **speaking** practice

Grammar reference

→ 6.1 Present Simple: *he/she/it* (1)

Positive

He She	gets up	at 8.00.
It	leaves	

→ 6.2 Spelling – Present Simple: *he/she/it*

1 Most verbs add -*s*.

He/She/It	listens leaves walks

2 Verbs ending in -*s*, -*ss*, -*sh*, -*ch* add -*es*.

He/She/It	watches washes

❶ *go*, *have*, and *do* are irregular.

He/She/It	***does*** ***goes*** ***has***

→ 6.3 Adverbs of frequency

0%	40%		90%	100%
never	sometimes		usually	always

Adverbs of frequency (*never*, *sometimes*, *usually*, *always*) can come before the verb.

*We **never** drink beer.*
*She **sometimes** goes out on a Saturday night.*
*He **usually** works late.*
*I **always** have tea for breakfast.*

→ 6.4 Present Simple: *he/she/it* (2)

Negative

He She	doesn't	**go out** in the evening. **eat** in a restaurant.

Questions with question words

What		he **have** for lunch?
Where	does	she **work**?
What time		he **go** to bed?
When		he **leave** work?

Yes/No questions and short answers

Does he **like** football?	Yes, he **does**. No, he **doesn't**.
Does she **speak** English?	Yes, she **does**. No, she **doesn't**.

❶ *Does he like tea?*   *Yes, he does.*   NOT ~~*Yes, he likes.*~~
Do you like coffee?   *No, I don't.*   NOT ~~*No, I don't like.*~~

Wordlist

adj = adjective	*n* = noun	*pl* = plural
adv = adverb	*phr* = phrase	*pron* = pronoun
conj = conjunction	*phr v* = phrasal verb	*v* = verb

always   *adv* /ˈɔːlweɪz/   _____
at the weekend   *phr* /ət ðə ˌwiːkˈend/   _____
breakfast   *n* /ˈbrekfəst/   _____
busy   *adj* /ˈbɪzi/   _____
buy   *v* /baɪ/   _____
cello   *n* /ˈtʃeləʊ/   _____
cook   *v* /kʊk/   _____
cycle   *v* /ˈsaɪkl/   _____
dinner   *n* /ˈdɪnə(r)/   _____
drive   *v* /draɪv/   _____
early   *adv* /ˈɜːli/   _____
egg   *n* /eg/   _____
exam   *n* /ɪɡˈzæm/   _____
fizzy drinks   *n pl* /ˈfɪzi drɪŋks/   _____
flat   *n* /flæt/   _____
flatmate   *n* /ˈflætmeɪt/   _____
fruit   *n* /fruːt/   _____
get home   *phr* /ˌɡet ˈhəʊm/   _____
get up   *phr v* /ˌɡet ˈʌp/   _____
go out   *phr v* /ˌɡəʊ ˈaʊt/   _____
go to bed   *phr* /ˌɡəʊ tə ˈbed/   _____
Good idea!   /ˌɡʊd aɪˈdiə/   _____
have a shower   *phr* /ˌhæv ə ˈʃaʊə(r)/   _____
hungry   *adj* /ˈhʌŋgri/   _____
in the week   *phr* /ˌɪn ðə ˈwiːk/   _____
late   *adv* /leɪt/   _____
leave   *v* /liːv/   _____
life   *n* /laɪf/   _____
lunch   *n* /lʌntʃ/   _____
never   *adv* /ˈnevə(r)/   _____
o' clock   *adv* /əˈklɒk/   _____
often   *adv* /ˈɒfn, ˈɒftən/   _____
park   *n* /pɑːk/   _____
relax   *v* /rɪˈlæks/   _____
salad   *n* /ˈsæləd/   _____
sausages   *n pl* /ˈsɒsɪdʒɪz/   _____
share   *v* /ʃeə(r)/   _____
shop assistant   *n* /ˈʃɒp əˌsɪstənt/   _____
stay   *v* /steɪ/   _____
takeaway   *n* /ˈteɪkəweɪ/   _____
tired   *adj* /ˈtaɪəd/   _____
toast   *n* /təʊst/   _____
typical   *adj* /ˈtɪpɪkl/   _____
usually   *adv* /ˈjuːʒuəli/   _____
visit   *n, v* /ˈvɪzɪt/   _____
walk   *n, v* /wɔːk/   _____
watch TV   *phr* /ˌwɒtʃ tiː ˈviː/   _____
When?   /wen/   _____
wrap   *n* /ræp/   _____

Days of the week
Monday   *n* /ˈmʌndeɪ/   _____
Tuesday   *n* /ˈtjuːzdeɪ/   _____
Wednesday   *n* /ˈwenzdeɪ/   _____
Thursday   *n* /ˈθɜːzdeɪ/   _____
Friday   *n* /ˈfraɪdeɪ/   _____
Saturday   *n* /ˈsætədeɪ/   _____
Sunday   *n* /ˈsʌndeɪ/   _____

Favourite things

7

- **Grammar** Question words; *me/him/us/them; this* and *that*
- **Vocabulary** Adjectives
- **Everyday English** *Can I...?*
- **Reading** An email from Dubai
- **Writing** A holiday email

Work with a partner. Answer the questions. ?

1 What is your favourite day of the week?

2 What do you do on that day?

Things I love!

1 What is your favourite … ?

> food   sport   drink   film   city

2 Ask and answer with a partner.

> What's your favourite food?

> I love pizza!

Grammar
Question words; *me/him/us/them*

1 Look at the photos. Who is Alfio Arcardi? Where is he from?

2 ◆)) 7.1 Look at the website 'The Chefs' Forum'. Read and listen. What is Alfio's favourite … ?

- olive oil
- city
- day

3 Complete the questions about Alfio.

1 _Where_ does he live?
2 _____ is he married to?
3 _____ old is their son?
4 _____ does his wife do?
5 _____ is his favourite chef?
6 _____ does he like cooking?
   Because …
7 _____ _____ restaurants do they have?
8 _____ do they relax?
9 _____ do they do in their free time?

4 Ask and answer the questions about Alfio with a partner.

> Where does he live?

> He lives in Tivoli, in Italy.

◆)) 7.2 Listen and compare.

THE CHEFS' *Forum*

Alfio Arcardi, top chef and owner of the Michelin star restaurant, *Buon Cibo* in Rome, answers your questions.

1 **KHRIS** from Stockholm
Your restaurant, Buon Cibo, is in the centre of Rome, but **where** do you live?

> **ALFIO** I live in Tivoli near Rome with my wife and son, Enzo. He's six. Tivoli is beautiful and quiet. I love it there. We have a house in the hills, it's our country home.

2 **JANE** from Manchester
I know your wife works in the restaurant, too. **What** does she do there?

> **ALFIO** Maria is a pastry chef. She's my best chef and my best friend. I love her very much and I think she loves me! We're very happy.

3 **SARAH** from Dublin
I have all your cookbooks and your recipes are fantastic. **What** olive oil do you use in your dishes?

> **ALFIO** Bramasole is my favourite olive oil. It's from Tuscany and it's perfect for cooking! Our friend, Pedro, works on the Bramasole estate. He delivers this amazing olive oil to us every month. He loves our restaurant.

4 **TURAN** from Istanbul
I have a lot of favourite chefs and I have all their cookbooks. **Who** are your favourite chefs?

> **ALFIO** Massimo Bottura, Locatelli, Giada De Laurentiis! I adore them all. But my favourite is Bottura. I really like him and his food. He's an amazing chef.

5 Read the text again. Complete the sentences with words from the website.

1 We have a house in the hills. It's _our_ country home. I love _it_ there.
2 She's my best friend. I love _____ very much, and I think she loves _____!
3 Pedro delivers oil to _____ every month. He likes _____ restaurant a lot.
4 Massimo Bottura, Locatelli, Giada De Laurentiis! I adore _____ all.
5 My brother's farm is near _____. We get fresh vegetables from _____.
6 We visit my brother and his family on _____ farm. _____ farm is beautiful.

6 Correct the information about Alfio. There are six mistakes including the example.

PROFILE

an Italian
Alfio is ~~a French~~ chef. He lives in Tivoli with his wife and daughter. He is a chef and the owner of the restaurant, Buon Cibo. Alfio's wife is a waitress at Buon Cibo. Alfio cooks with Bramasole olive oil from Tuscany. His friend, Pedro, delivers the oil to his restaurant every week. Alfio and his wife own three restaurants. Their favourite city is New York, and they want to open a Buon Cibo there one day. Saturday is their free day. They walk their dogs and visit Alfio's brother and his family at their beautiful farm.

◀)) **7.3** Listen and check. Read it aloud.

● **GRAMMAR SPOT**

Question words and pronouns

1 Match the question words with an answer.

Where?	Peter.
When?	In New York.
Who?	On Sunday.
Why?	Because …
How old?	Ten students.
How many?	Nearly seven.

2 Complete the chart.

Subject	I	you	he	she	it	we	they
Object	_me_	_you_	_him_			_us_	_them_
Possessive	_my_			_her_	_its_		

➔ Grammar reference 7.1–7.2 ▶ p70

▶ Go online to **watch** a video about a great place to shop.

---

5 **GEORGE** from Bucharest

I love cooking because my mother is an excellent cook. I'm 32 and she still cooks for me and my wife every Sunday. When my mum visits us, I like cooking for her. **Why** do you like cooking?

> **ALFIO** I like cooking because I love fresh food and we grow a lot of our food for the restaurant. My brother has a farm near us and we get a lot of fresh vegetables from him. Buon Cibo is a family business. I love my family and I love cooking for them.

6 **HELEN** from Sydney

A lot of famous chefs have restaurants around the world. **How many** restaurants do you have?

> **ALFIO** I have two. One in Rome and one in London. My favourite city is New York. I want to open a Buon Cibo there one day.

7 **EWAN** from Glasgow

Your life is very busy. **When** do you relax? **What** do you do in your free time?

> **ALFIO** Sunday is always our free day. It's our favourite day. We relax at our home in Tivoli. We walk our dogs and sometimes we visit my brother and his wife on their farm. We are very close to him and his lovely family. Their farm is beautiful.

this and *that*

This is my favourite

1 Look at the pictures. Complete the conversations with *this* or *that*.

1
A *This* is my favourite teddy bear.
B Ahhh. What's his name?
A Teddy!

2
A Wow! Who's _____ girl over there?
B It's my sister!
A She's beautiful!

3
A Look at _____ new app!
B That's cool. What is it?
A It's a Premier League app.

4
A How much is _____ bag?
B £85.99.
A Ahh! That's expensive.

5
A Look at _____!
B It's awful!
A I think it's amazing.

6
A Is _____ your coat?
B Yes. Thanks.
A My pleasure.

7
A I like _____ ring.
B The gold one?
A No, the diamond one!

8
A I like _____ wine. Where's it from?
B It's from England!
A Really?

9
A _____ is for you, Daddy.
B For me? Why?
A Because it's your birthday! Silly!

➔ Grammar reference 7.3 p70

🔊 **7.4** Listen and check. Practise the conversations.

2 Test the other students. Ask them questions about things in your classroom.

What's this in English?

It's a newspaper.

What's that in English?

It's a door.

Practice

I like you!

1 Complete the sentences with *you*, *her*, *it*, *us*, *them*.

| **1** | 'Do you like pizza?'<br>'Yes, I love _it_.' | **2** | 'Do you like cats?'<br>'No, I hate _____.' | **3** | 'Do you like me?'<br>'Yes, of course I like _____!' |

| **4** | 'Does your teacher teach you French?'<br>'No, she teaches _____ English.' | **5** | 'Do you like your teacher?'<br>'Yes, we like _____ very much.' |

🔊 **7.5** Listen and check.

Questions and answers

2 Work with a partner. Ask and answer the questions.

1 Why/you live in London? _Why do you live in London?_   (… like …)   _Because I like it._
2 Why/you/not eat tomatoes? _Why don't you eat tomatoes?_   (… hate …)   _____
3 Why/Annie want to marry Peter? _____   (… love …)   _____
4 Why/you eat so much chocolate? _____   (… adore …)   _____
5 Why/Dan always sit next to Sally? _____   (… like …)   _____
6 Why/you/not watch football? _____   (… hate …)   _____

🔊 **7.6** Listen and check.

➲ Grammar reference 7.4 p70

3 What do you like? Ask and answer questions with a partner. Ask about …

> football   golf   dogs   cats   Italian food   ice cream   pop music   coffee
> Mondays   video games   Facebook   your neighbours

Do you like golf?   Yes, I love it!   No, I hate it!

Do you like cats?   Oh yes! I adore them!

4 Match the questions and answers.

1 How do you come to school?	a They start at nine o'clock.
2 What do you have for breakfast?	b In an office in the centre of town.
3 Who's your favourite pop singer?	c By bus.
4 Where does your father work?	d I don't have a favourite.
5 Why do you want to learn English?	e Not a lot. About £5.
6 How much money do you have on you?	f Three.
7 What time do lessons start at your school?	g Because it's an international language.
8 How many languages does your teacher speak?	h Toast and coffee.

🔊 **7.7** Listen and check. Practise the questions.

Work with a partner. Ask and answer the questions about you.

⬈ Go online for more **grammar** practice

Vocabulary
Adjectives

1 Write the words.

1 The pizza is *d e l i c i o u s*. (LESICIUDO)
2 Your sister is really _ _ _ _. (CENI)
3 Our house is _ _ _ _ _ _ _. (VOLEYL)
4 It's the weekend. I'm really _ _ _ _ _. (APHYP)
5 Our English lessons are _ _ _ _ _ _ _ _ _ _ _ _. (NTIRSEGNTIE)
6 Paris is a _ _ _ _ _ _ _ _ _ _ city. (ETFLBAUIU)
7 Rain again! The weather is _ _ _ _ _. (FWAUL)
8 Ugh! This coffee is _ _ _ _ _ _ _ _ _ _ _. (DGUSIGINST)

2 Match the words and pictures.

old/new	expensive/cheap	~~big/small~~	hot/cold	right/wrong	dirty/clean

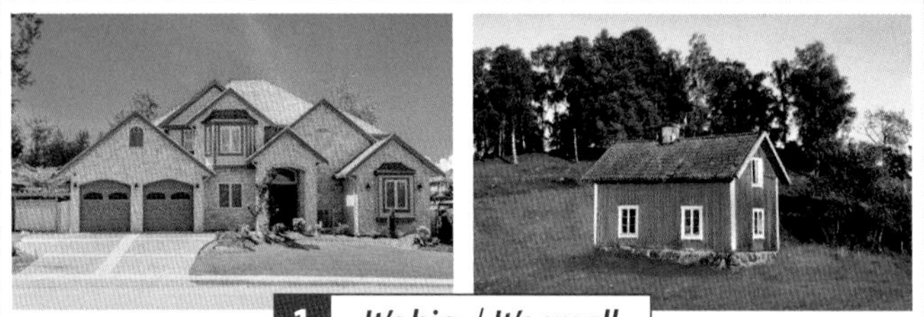

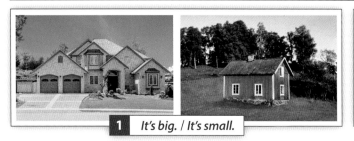

1 *It's big. / It's small.*

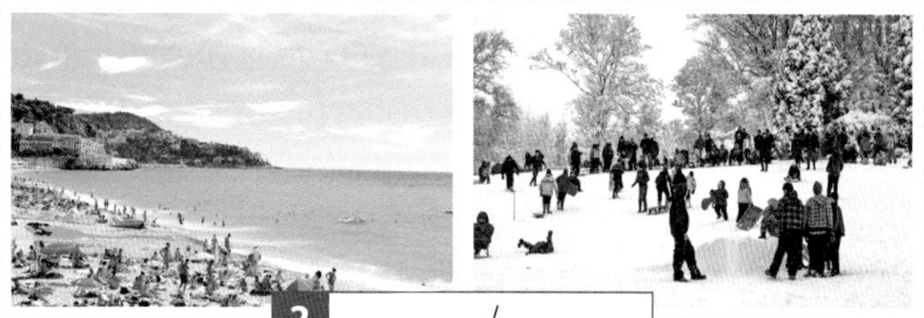

2 ______ / ______

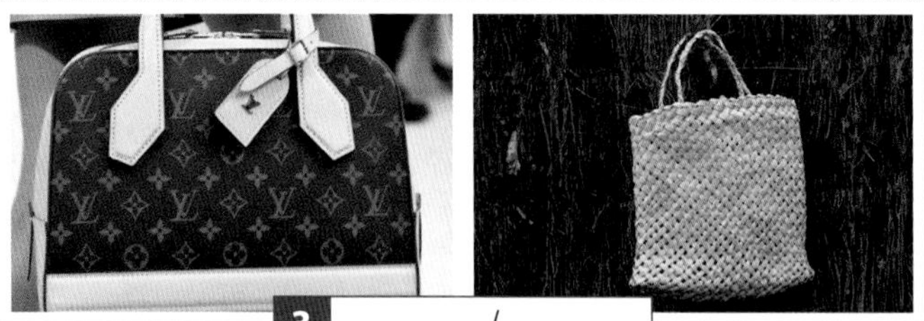

3 ______ / ______

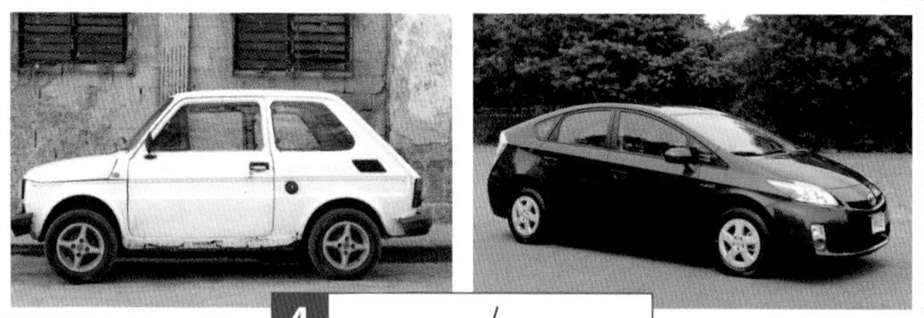

4 ______ / ______

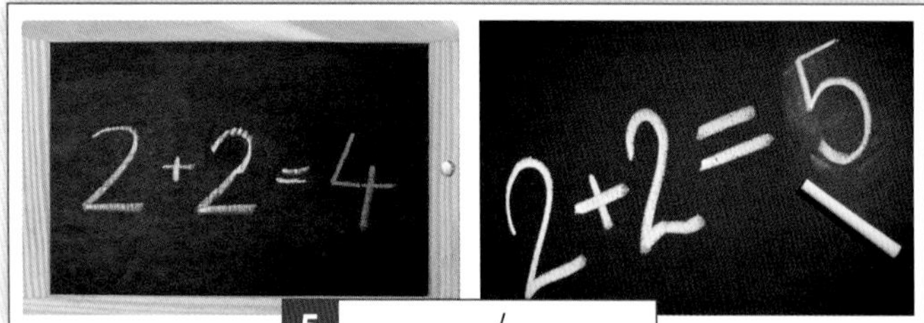

5 ______ / ______

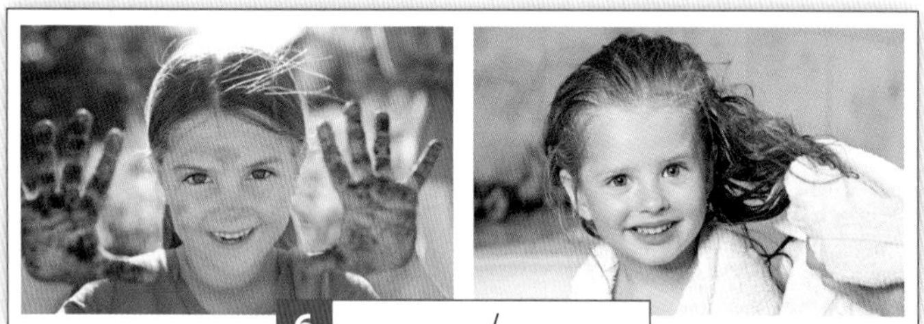

6 ______ / ______

3 7.8 Listen and complete the conversations.

1 **A** It's so *hot* today, isn't it?
B I know. It's ______ degrees!

2 **A** Hey! I like your ______ shoes!
B Thank you! They're really nice, aren't they?
A They're ______!

3 **A** I live in a very ______ apartment.
B ______ bedrooms do you have?
A Only one.

4 **A** ______ is that watch?
B £250.
A Wow! That's too ______ for me.

5 **A** Your name's Peter, isn't it?
B Yes, that's ______.
A ______ to meet you, Peter.

Practise the conversations with a partner.

Go online for more **vocabulary** practice

Reading and writing
An email from Dubai

1 🔊 7.9 Look at the email. Read and listen.

Hi Dom,

I'm on holiday in Dubai this month. Our hotel is fantastic – really new and comfortable, and really near the Burj Al Arab. I'm here with my best friend, Helen. She's really nice and funny.

The food is international and delicious. I like all the restaurants at the hotel, but the Indian restaurant is my favourite. It's wonderful!

Dubai is an interesting place – very modern. It's really hot – too hot to walk – we always travel by car. All the buildings are so big and tall. The Burj Khalifa has 163 floors! The view is amazing – you can see all the way to the sand of the desert. The shops are great, but very expensive.

There are no green parks, but there are lovely golden beaches, and we love swimming here.

This is a super holiday. It's great in Dubai!

See you soon.

Love,

Louise

Burj Khalifa

Burj Al Arab

2 Answer the questions.
1 Who is the email from?
2 Where is she?
3 Who is she with?
4 Why are they in Dubai?
5 What isn't good about the shops?
6 Is their holiday good?

3 What adjectives does Louise use?

	Adjectives		
their hotel	*fantastic*	_____	*comfortable*
Helen	_____	_____	
food	_____	_____	
Indian restaurant	_____		
Dubai	_____	_____	_____
buildings	_____	_____	
shops	_____	_____	
beaches	_____	_____	

Writing

4 You're on holiday. Write an email to a friend.

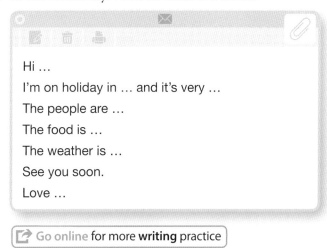

Hi …

I'm on holiday in … and it's very …

The people are …

The food is …

The weather is …

See you soon.

Love …

↗ Go online for more **writing** practice

Everyday English

Can I …?

1 Write a number **1–5** (place) and a letter **a–e** (activity) for each photo.

<table>
<tr><td>

PLACES

1 a chemist's
2 a railway station
3 a post office
4 a clothes shop
5 a café

</td><td>

ACTIVITIES

a have a coffee
b buy some aspirin
c post letters
d catch a train
e try on a jumper

</td></tr>
</table>

2 | d

Iveta in town

2 🔊 **7.10** Listen to Iveta. She is in different places in town. Where is she in the conversations? What does she want?

Where is she?	What does she want?
1 *at the railway station*	*a return ticket to Oxford*
2	
3	
4	
5	

3 Complete the conversations with a partner.

---

1 AT A RAILWAY STATION

I Can I have a return ¹_____ to Oxford, please?
A Sure.
I How much ²_____ _____?
A Twenty-two ³_____ fifty, please.
I Can I ⁴_____ by ⁵_____ card?
A No problem. Put your card in the machine and enter your PIN number, please.

---

2 IN A CLOTHES SHOP

I Hello. Can I ¹_____ _____ this jumper, please?
B ²_____ _____. The changing rooms are over there.

---

3 IN A POST OFFICE

I ¹_____ _____ post this parcel to the Netherlands, ²_____?
C Sure. Put it on the scales. That's £8.55.
I Thank you. ³_____ _____ is a stamp for a postcard to the United States?
C One pound ⁴_____ - _____.
I Can I have ⁵_____, please?

---

4 IN A CAFÉ

D Yes, please!
I Can I have a ¹_____, please? A latte.
D Large or small?
I ²_____, _____. To take away.
D Sure. Anything to eat?
I No, ³_____ _____. Just a coffee.
D Thanks ⁴_____ _____.

---

5 IN A CHEMIST'S

E Next, please!
I Hello. Can I have ¹_____ aspirin, please?
E Twelve or twenty-four?
I Pardon?
E Do you ²_____ a packet of twelve or twenty-four?
I Oh, twelve's ³_____, thanks.

🔊 **7.11** Listen and check. Practise the conversations.

Role-play

4 Work with a partner. Make more conversations with different information.

- a return/single ticket to Newcastle/London
- this jacket/T-shirt
- this parcel to Spain/this letter to Australia
- a cheese and salad sandwich/an ice cream
- shampoo/toothpaste

[➦ Go online for more **speaking** practice]

Grammar reference

→ **7.1 Question words**

What?	A hamburger.	**How?**	By taxi.
When?	In the evening.	**How old?**	16.
What time?	At 8.00.	**How many?**	Two.
Who?	Peter.	**How much?**	$2.
Where?	In Paris.	**Why?**	Because …

→ **7.2 Pronouns**

Subject pronouns	I	you	he	she	it	we	they
Object pronouns	me	you	him	her	it	us	them
Possessive adjectives	my	your	his	her	its	our	their

She loves **him**.

I like **your** car.

→ **7.3 *this/that***

We use *this* to refer to things near to us.

This is my son.   I like **this** sandwich.

We use *that* to refer to things that are not near to us.

That's my house.   I don't like **that** car.

→ **7.4 Negative questions**

Why	**don't**	I you we they	eat tomatoes?
	doesn't	he she	

Wordlist

adj = adjective	*det* = determiner	*phr v* = phrasal verb
adv = adverb	*excl* = exclamation	*pl* = plural
conj = conjunction	*n* = noun	*v* = verb

app *n* /æp/	_____
aspirin *n* /ˈæsprɪn/	_____
beach *n* /biːtʃ/	_____
because *conj* /bɪˈkɒz/	_____
bedroom *n* /ˈbedruːm/	_____
catch *v* /kætʃ/	_____
changing rooms *n pl* /ˈtʃeɪndʒɪŋ ˌruːmz/	_____
cheap *adj* /tʃiːp/	_____
chemist's *n* /ˈkemɪsts/	_____
clean *adj* /kliːn/	_____
close *adj* /kləʊs/	_____
clothes *n pl* /kləʊðz/	_____
cold *adj* /kəʊld/	_____
comfortable *adj* /ˈkʌmftəbl/	_____
deliver *v* /dɪˈlɪvə(r)/	_____
desert *n* /ˈdezət/	_____
dirty *adj* /ˈdɜːti/	_____
door *n* /dɔː(r)/	_____
excellent *adj* /ˈeksələnt/	_____
expensive *adj* /ɪkˈspensɪv/	_____
free time *n* /ˌfriː ˈtaɪm/	_____
fresh *adj* /freʃ/	_____
hate *v* /heɪt/	_____
hot *adj* /hɒt/	_____
How many? /ˌhaʊ ˈmeni/	_____
Indian *adj* /ˈɪndiən/	_____
international *adj* /ˌɪntəˈnæʃnəl/	_____
jumper *n* /ˈdʒʌmpə(r)/	_____
large *adj* /lɑːdʒ/	_____
money *n* /ˈmʌni/	_____
month *n* /mʌnθ/	_____
nice *adj* /naɪs/	_____
old *adj* /əʊld/	_____
olive oil *n* /ˈɒlɪv ˌɔɪl/	_____
owner *n* /ˈəʊnə(r)/	_____
packet *n* /ˈpækɪt/	_____
parcel *n* /ˈpɑːsl/	_____
Pardon? *excl* /ˈpɑːdn/	_____
post *v* /pəʊst/	_____
post office *n* /ˈpəʊst ˌɒfɪs/	_____
postcard *n* /ˈpəʊstkɑːd/	_____
quiet *adj* /ˈkwaɪət/	_____
railway station *n* /ˈreɪlweɪ ˌsteɪʃn/	_____
recipe *n* /ˈresəpi/	_____
return ticket *n* /rɪˈtɜːn ˌtɪkɪt/	_____
right *adj* /raɪt/	_____
sand *n* /sænd/	_____
single ticket *n* /ˈsɪŋgl ˌtɪkɪt/	_____
stamp *n* /stæmp/	_____
teach *v* /tiːtʃ/	_____
teddy bear *n* /ˈtedi beə(r)/	_____
that *det* /ðæt/	_____
train *n* /treɪn/	_____
try on *phr v* /traɪ ˈɒn/	_____
Who? /huː/	_____
Why? /waɪ/	_____
wonderful *adj* /ˈwʌndəfl/	_____
wrong *adj* /rɒŋ/	_____

Home sweet home 8

Work with a partner. Answer the questions.

1 Do you live in a house or a flat?

2 Do you have a garden?

 Watch the video introduction online

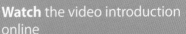 Use your **Workbook** for self study

 Go online for more practice and to *Check your Progress*

My house

STARTER

🔊 **8.1** Look at the picture of the house. Listen and repeat the names of the rooms.

Grammar

There is/There are

1 Find the things in the house. Write the letters.

_b_ a bed	___ a lamp	___ a shower
___ a laptop	___ an armchair	___ a TV
___ a PlayStation	___ a fridge	___ a sofa
___ a magazine	___ a table	___ a cooker
___ a picture	___ a toilet	___ a desk

🔊 **8.2** Listen, check and repeat.

2 🔊 **8.3** Look at the house. Listen and repeat.

There's a cooker.	There are two armchairs.
There's a sofa.	There are two TVs.

Talk to a partner about the things in the rooms.

> There's a PlayStation.

> There are six pictures.

↪ Go online for more **vocabulary** practice

There is/isn't, There are/aren't

Two student flats

1 ◀)) 8.4 Listen to Jack and Sophie's descriptions of their flats. Match them with the pictures.

Jack   Sophie

A _____'s flat.

B _____'s flat.

2 Work in pairs.

Student A read and complete Flat A

Student B read and complete Flat B

A My flat isn't very big, but because my kitchen and living room are one room, it feels big. I love it! ¹***There's*** a blue sofa, and ²_____ two old armchairs. ³_____ a small kitchen table. I always have a bowl of fruit on it. ⁴_____ four chairs round the table. I'm an artist, so ⁵_____ a lot of my pictures on the walls. ⁶_____ also lots of art books and magazines on the table and the floor! It's not very tidy, but I think it's great. It's my home.

B 'I have a really cool flat. ⁷_____ a great view of the park. My living room is big and comfortable. ⁸_____ two new large black sofas and my favourite old armchair. ⁹_____ a coffee table with a PlayStation on it, and ¹⁰_____ a huge TV on the wall and ¹¹_____ a lot of posters of David Bowie – he's my hero! ¹²_____ also a desk with a lamp on it – my living room is my study too.

◀)) 8.4 Listen again and check.

3 Talk to your partner about the rooms.

> In _____'s room there's a blue sofa.

> Oh, in _____'s room there are two large black sofas!

4 ◀)) 8.5 Listen and repeat the questions and answers.

Sophie's flat	Jack's flat
Is there a sofa?	**Is there** a kitchen table?
✓ Yes, there is.	✗ No, there isn't.
Are there any pictures?	**Are there** any books?
✓ Yes, there are.	✗ No, there aren't.

5 Work in pairs. Ask and answer questions about the things in flats A and B.

- a phone
- a laptop
- a PlayStation
- a desk
- a cooker
- a fruit bowl
- a fridge
- posters
- books
- magazines
- armchairs
- photos

> Is there a phone?

> No, there isn't.

Talking about you

6 Ask and answer questions about your partner's house or flat.

> Is there a TV in your bedroom?

● GRAMMAR SPOT

Complete the sentences.

Positive There's a sofa. _____ _____ two armchairs.

Questions _____ there a TV? _____ **there** any pictures?

Negative There isn't a bed. **There** _____ any books.

→ Grammar reference 8.1 ⟩ p80

Prepositions; *some/any*

Jack's bedroom

1 Look at the prepositions.

in	on		next to
		under	

➔ Grammar reference 8.2 **p80**

2 Look at Jack's bedroom. Write a preposition from exercise 1.

1 Jack's cap is __*on*__ the bed.
2 His trainers are _____ the bed.
3 There are some sports magazines _____ the floor _____ his bed.
4 His car keys are _____ the drawer.
5 There's a football _____ the floor _____ the chair.
6 There are some credit cards _____ the bedside table _____ his bed.

🔊 **8.6** Listen and check. Practise the sentences.

● GRAMMAR SPOT

Positive	There are **some** magazines.
Questions	Are there **any** magazines?
Negative	There aren't **any** books.

➔ Grammar reference 8.3 ▶ **p80**

3 Ask and answer questions with a partner about Jack's things.

> Where's Jack's cap?
> It's on the bed.

> Where are his car keys?
> They're in the drawer.

Ask about his …
- sports bag
- pens
- lamp
- jeans
- boots
- magazines
- chocolate
- coffee cup
- trainers

▶ Go online to **watch** a video about an interesting home.

A phone call with Jack's mum

4 🔊 8.7 Listen to Jack talking to his mother. Tick (✓) the things she asks about.

- [✓] sofa
- [ ] TV
- [ ] pictures
- [ ] table
- [ ] lamp
- [ ] posters
- [ ] chairs
- [ ] desk

5 🔊 8.7 Listen again. Answer the questions.

1 What does she like about the flat? What doesn't she like? Why?

2 When does she want to visit? Does Jack want her to visit?

Practice

Questions and answers

1 Put the words in the correct order to make questions.

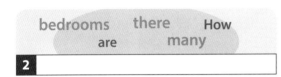

house   Do   live   **or**   you
flat   a   in   a

1   Do you live in a house or a flat?

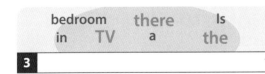

bedrooms   there   How
are   many

2

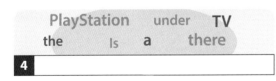

bedroom   there   Is
in   TV   a   the

3

PlayStation   under   **TV**
the   Is   a   there

4

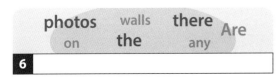

living   books   a lot of   in
Are   there   room   your

5

photos   walls   **there**   Are
on   **the**   any

6

🔊 8.8 Listen and check.

2 Work with a partner. Ask and answer questions about where you live.

Two different kitchens

3 Work with a partner.

Student A Look at the picture on this page.
Student B Look at the picture on p141.
Your pictures are different. Talk about your pictures to find seven differences.

4 🔊 8.9 Listen to a description of one of the kitchens. Which one is it?

5 Close your eyes! Ask and answer questions about things in the classroom.

Where's Emma's phone?   It's on her desk.

Check it

6 Tick (✓) the correct sentence.

1 [ ] Is a sofa in the living room?
  [ ] Is there a sofa in the living room?

2 [ ] There's PlayStation under the TV.
  [ ] There's a PlayStation under the TV.

3 [ ] Are there a poster on the wall?
  [ ] Are there any posters on the wall?

4 [ ] The table is next the bed.
  [ ] The table is next to the bed.

5 [ ] Is there a cat on the bed?
  [ ] Is there any cat on the bed?

🔗 Go online for more **grammar** practice

Reading and vocabulary
Cape Town – BEST place in the world!

1 Work with a partner. Look at the map of Africa. Where is Cape Town?

2 Look at the photos. Find these things.
- a bus
- penguins
- a vineyard
- a beach
- a campsite
- seafood
- a ferry
- a train
- a mountain

3 Read the text about Cape Town. Write the five paragraph headings in the correct place.

~~Where is it?~~ What to do

Where to stay How to travel

When to go Where to eat

🔊 8.10 Listen and check.

4 Answer the questions.
1 Where in South Africa is Cape Town?
2 When is a good time to visit? Why?
3 When is the best time for a beach holiday?
4 What do people do … ?
- on the beach
- at vineyards
- at the Victoria and Albert Waterfront
5 Why is the seafood so delicious?
6 Are all the hotels expensive?
7 Why is Cape Town a nice place to go camping?
8 What is a good way to see the city?

5 Complete the chart with adjectives from the text.

Adjectives	Nouns
famous, spectacular, amazing	Table Mountain
	weather
	beaches
	penguins
	vineyards
	night life
	city
	seafood
	hotels
	buses
	trains

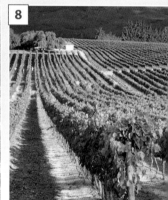
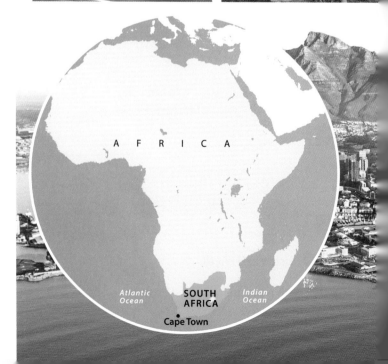

Cape Town, South Africa

'Best place to visit in the world!' *The New York Times*

Why? Wonderful views, fabulous beaches, friendly people and a cosmopolitan culture. It is the number one place to visit!

Where is it?

Cape Town is on the south-west coast of South Africa, below the famous and spectacular Table Mountain, named one of the Seven Wonders of Nature.

It is always a good time to visit Cape Town. The weather is warm and sunny most of the year. The best time for a beach holiday is at Christmas!

Walk up the amazing Table Mountain, sunbathe on the fabulous, sandy beaches and swim with the friendly penguins. Visit the excellent vineyards and drink some of the best wine in the world. Go shopping at the Victoria and Albert Waterfront – it's fantastic! For exciting nightlife, the city also has bars, clubs, cinemas and theatres. Cape Town is a lot of fun!

Cape Town is a cosmopolitan city. There are Italian, Turkish, Japanese, Indian and French restaurants, and many more! It is by the sea, so there is a lot of delicious fresh seafood. Also, because of the lovely weather, there is a lot of fresh fruit and vegetables too, so the restaurants have the best ingredients. South Africans love their food.

There are cheap hotels near the airport, but for a really cheap holiday, stay at one of Cape Town's excellent campsites. The weather is warm, so a night in a tent is fun! For a five-star holiday, stay at one of the expensive but very comfortable hotels on the Waterfront. They have wonderful views.

You don't need a car in Cape Town. The MyCiTi buses are new and fast and go everywhere. There is also the Metrorail train, but this is slow and sometimes late. Take the ferry to the famous Robben Island for a really exciting day.

Listening and writing
My home town

1 🔊 8.11 Listen to Ben. He lives in Cape Town. Tick (✓) the things he talks about.

- ☐ his job
- ☐ seafood
- ☐ his brother
- ☐ sunbathing
- ☐ the weather
- ☐ his girlfriend
- ☐ Boulders Beach
- ☐ football
- ☐ his friends
- ☐ French food
- ☐ kitesurfing
- ☐ penguins

2 🔊 8.11 Listen again. Answer the questions.

1 Where does Ben live?
2 Where does he work?
3 Is his apartment big?
4 What is his favourite food?
5 Why does he like the wind?
6 Does he have a pet?
7 What sports does he like?
8 When and where does he cycle?

3 🔊 8.12 Listen to four conversations with Ben. Complete the table.

	Where is Ben?	Who is he talking to?
1		
2		
3		
4		

Talking about you

4 In groups, talk about your home town.
- Where do you live?
- What is there in your town?
- What do you do there with your friends?
- Where do you go shopping?
- How do you travel?
- Is it a good place to live?

Writing

5 Write about a town you know.

Where is it?	… is a town in …
When to visit?	The best time to visit is …
What to do?	Go … There are a lot of …
Where to eat?	There are good restaurants in … My favourite restaurant is …
Where to stay?	… is an expensive hotel in … … is a cheap hotel near/next to …
How to travel?	The best way to see the town is …

Read your description to your partner.

⤴ Go online for more writing practice

Everyday English
Directions

1 Find the places on the map.

> hotel bank chemist's pub railway station the Beach Café cinema
> square newsagent's church supermarket football stadium campsite
> restaurant surf school fish and chip shop garden centre souvenir shop

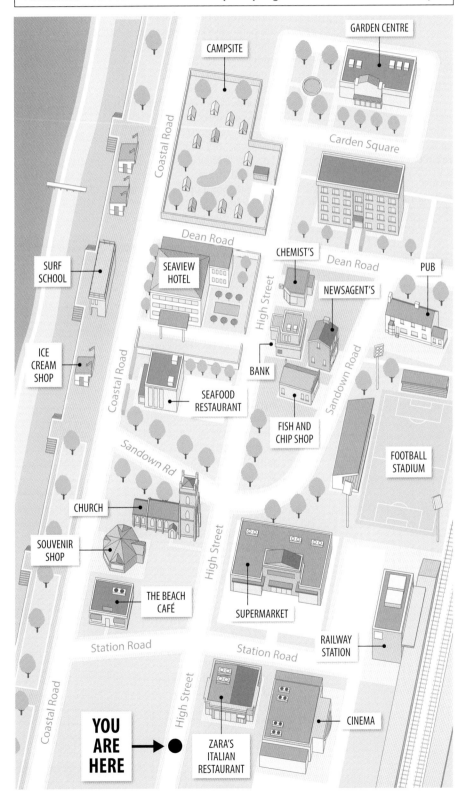

2 What do the signs mean?

> turn right   go straight on   turn left

Ⓐ Ⓑ Ⓒ

_____ _____ _____

3 🔊 8.13 Listen to the directions. Start from YOU ARE HERE on the map. Follow the directions. Where are you?

1 Go up the High Street. Turn right into Station Road. It's on the right next to the Italian restaurant.
   at the cinema _____

2 _____

3 _____

4 _____

5 _____

6 _____

Look at audioscript 8.13 on page 143. Practise the directions.

4 Work with a partner. Have similar conversations. Ask about …

- a pub
- a campsite
- a football stadium
- a bank
- a chemist's
- an Italian restaurant

> Excuse me, is there a … near here?

> Yes. Go down …

Talking about you

5 With your partner, ask for and give directions to places in your town.

> How do I get to the station?

> Go out of the school, turn right …

> Is it far?   About ten minutes.

> 📲 Go online for more **speaking** practice

Grammar reference

➔ 8.1 *There is/There are*

Positive

There's *a sofa in the living room.*
   (There's = There is)
There are *two bedrooms in my house.*

Negative

There isn't *a TV.*
There aren't *any photos.*

Questions

Is there *a TV in the kitchen?*
Are there *any magazines on the table?*
*How many lamps **are there**?*

Short answers

Is there a TV in the bedroom?	Yes, **there is.** No, **there isn't.**
Are there any photos on the wall?	Yes, **there are.** No, **there aren't.**

➔ 8.2 Prepositions

in The credit cards are **in** the drawer.

on There's a lamp **on** the bedside table.

The trainers are **under** the bed.
under

next to There are some photos **next to** the books.

➔ 8.3 *some* and *any*

We use *some* in positive sentences.

*There are **some** books.*

We use *any* in questions and negatives.

*Does he have **any** photos?*
*There aren't **any** lamps.*

See 12.2 on p120 for more information on *some* and *any*.

Wordlist

adj = adjective	*n* = noun	*prep* = preposition
adv = adverb	*phr* = phrase	*pron* = pronoun
conj = conjunction	*pl* = plural	*v* = verb

armchair   *n* /ˈɑːmtʃeə(r)/ _____
artist   *n* /ˈɑːtɪst/ _____
bank   *n* /bæŋk/ _____
bathroom   *n* /ˈbɑːruːm/ _____
campsite   *n* /ˈkæmpsaɪt/ _____
car park   *n* /ˈkɑː ˌpɑːk/ _____
chair   *n* /tʃeə(r)/ _____
church   *n* /tʃɜːtʃ/ _____
cinema   *n* /ˈsɪnəmə/ _____
cooker   *n* /ˈkʊkə(r)/ _____
cosmopolitan   *adj* /kɒzməˈpɒlɪtən/ _____
desk   *n* /desk/ _____
drawer   *n* /drɔː(r)/ _____
fabulous   *adj* /ˈfæbjələs/ _____
far   *adj* /fɑː(r)/ _____
fast   *adj* /fɑːst/ _____
fish and chip shop   *n* /ˌfɪʃ ənd ˈtʃɪp ʃɒp/ _____
floor   *n* /flɔː(r)/ _____
football stadium   *n* /ˈfʊtbɔːl ˌsteɪdiəm/ _____
fridge   *n* /frɪdʒ/ _____
furniture   *n* /ˈfɜːnɪtʃə(r)/ _____
garden centre   *n* /ˈgɑːdn ˌsentə(r)/ _____
go shopping   *phr* /ˌgəʊ ˈʃɒpɪŋ/ _____
huge   *adj* /hjuːdʒ/ _____
kitchen   *n* /ˈkɪtʃn/ _____
kitesurfing   *n* /ˈkaɪtsɜːfɪŋ/ _____
lamp   *n* /læmp/ _____
living room   *n* /ˈlɪvɪŋ ˌruːm/ _____
magazine   *n* /ˌmægəˈziːn/ _____
minute   *n* /ˈmɪnɪt/ _____
mountain   *n* /ˈmaʊntən/ _____
newsagent's   *n* /ˈnjuːzeɪdʒənts/ _____
next to   *prep* /ˈnekst tuː, tə/ _____
pen   *n* /pen/ _____
penguin   *n* /ˈpeŋgwɪn/ _____
picture   *n* /ˈpɪktʃə(r)/ _____
poster   *n* /ˈpəʊstə(r)/ _____
room   *n* /ruːm/ _____
sea   *n* /siː/ _____
seafood   *n* /ˈsiːfuːd/ _____
slow   *adj* /sləʊ/ _____
sofa   *n* /ˈsəʊfə/ _____
souvenir shop   *n* /ˌsuːvəˈnɪə(r) ʃɒp/ _____
square   *n* /skweə(r)/ _____
straight on   *adv* /ˌstreɪt ɒn/ _____
study   *n* /ˈstʌdi/ _____
sunbathe   *v* /ˈsʌnbeɪð/ _____
table   *n* /ˈteɪbl/ _____
theatre   *n* /ˈθɪətə(r)/ _____
tidy   *adj* /ˈtaɪdi/ _____
turn   *v* /tɜːn/ _____
under   *prep* /ˈʌndə(r)/ _____
vineyard   *n* /ˈvɪnjəd/ _____
wall   *n* /wɔːl/ _____
wind   *n* /wɪnd/ _____
wonder   *n* /ˈwʌndə(r)/ _____

Past times

9

- **Grammar** Past Simple – *was/were*; Irregular verbs
- **Vocabulary** Saying years; Common verbs (2): *have, do, go*
- **Everyday English** Months and dates
- **Reading** The lottery ticket

Old street scene

Look at the photo. What can you see?
There's a tram.

 Watch the video introduction online

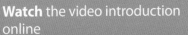 Use your **Workbook** for self study

 Go online for more practice and to *Check your Progress*

When was he born?

1 **9.1** Listen and repeat.

1840 eighteen forty	**1996** nineteen ninety-six
2005 two thousand and five	**2017** twenty seventeen

2 **9.2** Listen and underline the years you hear.

1 1696 / 1686   2 1916 / 1960   3 2004 / 2014   4 1699 / 1799   5 1840 / 1945   6 2017 / 2071

3 What year is it now? What year was it last year? What year is it next year?

Grammar
was/were born

1 Look at the photos. Do you know the people? When were they born?

9.3 Listen and write the years.

Steve Jobs, the inventor of Apple Computers, was born in _____ in San Francisco, California.

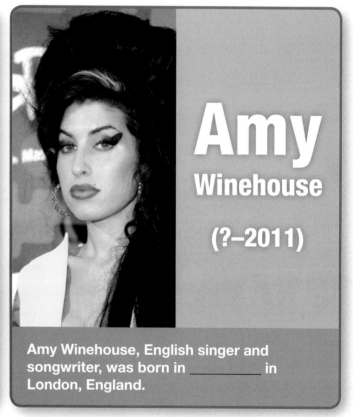

Amy Winehouse, English singer and songwriter, was born in _____ in London, England.

2 **9.4** Listen and repeat.

He was an inventor. He was born in …
She was a singer and songwriter. She was born in …

3 Ask and answer questions with other students.

> How old are you?

> I'm 17. I was born in 20…

4 **9.5** Listen to the questions and answers. Practise them.

When **were** you born?	I was born in 1996.
When **was** he born?	He was born in 1983.
When **was** she born?	She was born in 2000.
When **were** they born?	They were born in 2003.

Complete the chart of the verb *to be*.

	Present	Past
I	am	was
You	are	
He/She/It	is	
We	are	were
They	are	

 **9.6** Listen and repeat.

→ Grammar reference 9.1 〉 p90

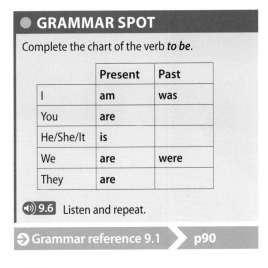

ROLF ACKMAN
MY FAMILY

Sarah
_____

Bert   Karen
_____   _____

Rolf   Susan   Barney   Lottie
1999   _____   _____   _____

5 **9.7** This is Rolf Ackman. Listen to him talking about his family. Write when the people were born.

6 Work with a partner. Ask and answer questions about Rolf's family.

> Who's Susan? | She's Rolf's sister.

> When was she born? | In …

> Who are Bert and Karen? | They're his …

> When were they … ?

Talking about you

7 Write the names of some people in your family.

Peter   Olivia

Work with a partner. Ask and answer questions about them.

> Who's Peter? | He's my grandfather.

> When was he born? | I'm not sure. I think about 1948.

8 Tell the class about your partner's family.
Simon's grandfather was born in 1948. His mother was born in 1969.

 Go online to **watch** a video about Steve Jobs.

Practice

Who were they?

1 Who are the people in the photos? Match the people **1–9** and the jobs in the box.

☐ princess	☐ explorer
☐ boxer	☐ politician
☐ scientist	☐ writer
1 astronaut	☐ architect
☐ actor	

2 9.8 Listen and write when they were born.

3 9.9 Listen and repeat the questions and answers.

> **Who was Neil Armstrong?** ?
> He was an astronaut.
> **Where was he born?**
> In Ohio, in the US.
> **When was he born?**
> In 1930.

Work with a partner. Ask and answer the questions about the other people.

Who was Nelson Mandela?

He was a …

Negatives and pronunciation

4 Complete the sentences.

A Steve Jobs was an architect.
B No, he wasn't. He was an ________.

A Steve Jobs and Neil Armstrong were English.
B No, they weren't. They were ________.

9.10 Listen and repeat.

GRAMMAR SPOT

1 The negative of **was** is **wasn't** (= was not)
The negative of **were** is **weren't** (= were not)

2 9.11 Listen and repeat.

1
/wəz/
A He was an architect.
/'wɒznt/
B No, he wasn't.

2
/wə/
A They were English.
/wɜːnt/
B No, they weren't.

Grammar reference 9.1 p90

?–2011

1 **Neil Armstrong** was born in *1930* in Ohio, in the US.

?–1997

2 **Diana Spencer** was born in ________, in Sandringham, England.

?–2013

4 **Nelson Mandela** was born in ________, in Mvezo, South Africa.

?–2016

5 **Muhammad Ali** was born in ________, in Louisville, in the US.

?–1910

7 **Leo Tolstoy** was born in ________, in Yasnaya Polyana, Russia.

?–2016

8 **Carrie Fisher** was born in ________, in California, in the US.

?–2016

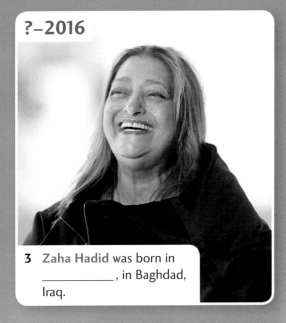

3 **Zaha Hadid** was born in
_____ , in Baghdad,
Iraq.

?–1506

6 **Christopher Columbus**
was born in _____ ,
in Genoa, Italy.

?–1934

9 **Marie Curie** was born in
_____ , in Warsaw,
Poland.

5 Correct the information.

1 Christopher Columbus was a scientist.
No, he _**wasn't**_ ! _He was an explorer_ !

2 Zaha Hadid was a princess.
No, she _____ ! _____ !

3 Marie Curie was born in 1919.
No, she _____ ! _____ !

4 Diana Spencer and Amy Winehouse were born in the US.
No, they _____ ! _____ !

5 Nelson Mandela and Neil Armstrong were both politicians.
No, they _____ ! Mandela _____ a politician, but Armstrong _____ !

6 Leo Tolstoy was an Italian actor.
No, he _____ ! _____ !

🔊 **9.12** Listen and check. Practise with a partner.

Today and yesterday

6 What is true for you? Tell a partner.

Today is …	Monday / Tuesday / Wednesday …
Yesterday was …	
Today I'm …	at school / at home / at work …
Yesterday I was …	
Today the weather is …	hot / cold / wet / lovely / horrible …
Yesterday the weather was …	
Today my parents are …	at home / at work …
Yesterday my parents were …	

Check it

7 Complete the sentences with *was*, *wasn't*, *were*, or *weren't*.

1 Where _**was**_ your mother born?

2 When _____ your parents born?

3 My parents _____ born in 1965. My father was born in 1962, and my mother in 1967.

4 No, I _____ on holiday in Barcelona in 2015.

5 '_____ he at home yesterday?'
'No, he _____.'

6 '_____ you at work yesterday?'
'Yes, we _____.'

7 '_____ they at school yesterday morning?'
'No, they _____.'

⤷ **Go online** for more **grammar** practice

Reading and speaking
Past Simple – irregular verbs

1 Match the present and the past forms of the verbs. Look at the *Irregular verbs* list on the inside front cover of your Student's Book.

Present	Past
be	bought /bɔːt/
buy	had
go	made
have	put
make	was/were
put	went
run	sat
see	saw
sit	ran

🔊 9.13 Listen and check. Practise the verbs.

➔ Grammar reference 9.2 p90

2 Look at the pictures. They tell a story. Where is the woman? Who is the little boy?

Match sentences **a–f** with the pictures **1–6**.

a On Saturday night, Tina made a cup of tea and sat on the sofa to watch the lottery on TV. She was amazed to see her numbers.

b She was angry with her grandson because he ran round the shop and made a lot of noise.

c She went to the washing machine. The lottery ticket was in the pocket of her clean jeans! But, oh dear! The ticket was clean too – there were no numbers on it!

d She bought a ticket and put it in the back pocket of her jeans.

e Last Saturday, Tina Green went to her local newsagent's with her grandson to buy a lottery ticket. The jackpot was an amazing £35 million.

f She went to get her bag and check her lottery ticket. The ticket wasn't there!

3 Read and complete the news article with the irregular verbs from exercise 1.

The Lottery Ticket

Oh no! What bad luck!!

Last Saturday, Tina Green, a 56-year-old grandmother from Cambridge in England, [1] *went* to her local newsagent's and [2]_____ a lottery ticket for £2. She was very excited because this week the jackpot was £35 million! Every Saturday Tina plays the same numbers, and she always puts her ticket in her bag. But this Saturday she [3]_____ her small grandson, Billy, with her. 'He was a little monkey!', said Tina. 'He [4]_____ round the shop and [5]_____ a lot of noise.' She was so busy with him that she [6]_____ the ticket in the back pocket of her jeans.

The lottery is on TV every Saturday evening, and Tina loves watching it. 'It's really exciting. I love listening for my numbers – they're my lucky numbers, well … they [7]_____ my lucky numbers!'

Last Saturday, Tina made a cup of tea and [8]_____ on the sofa to watch the lottery. One by one, she [9]_____ her numbers on the TV. She was amazed – all the numbers were on her ticket. She was very excited, and she went to find the ticket in her bag, but the ticket wasn't there. It [10]_____ in her jeans' pocket, and her jeans were in the washing machine. Her jeans were clean and so was the ticket! There were no numbers on it. No numbers – no £35 million!

4 🔊 9.14 Listen and check. Read the article aloud to a partner.

5 Look at the pictures only and tell the story again.

Vocabulary
Common verbs (2): *have, do, go*

1 Look at the words that go with *have, do* and *go*.

They **have lunch** at 1.00.

I always **do** my **homework** with my dad.

I **go shopping** with my friends on Saturday afternoons.

2 Write the words in the box next to the correct verb, *have, do* or *go*.

~~shopping~~	~~my homework~~	~~lunch~~
a shower	the housework	on holiday
for a walk	some exercise	home
a good time	breakfast	to work

lunch

have _____

_____

_____

my homework

do _____

_____

_____

shopping

go _____

_____

_____

_____

3 Write the past of *have, do* and *go*.

went   had   did

Present	Past
have	
do	
go	

4 Complete the sentences with *went, had* or *did*.

1 Yesterday I met my husband at one o'clock and we **had** lunch in a restaurant.

2 I hate doing housework, but last Sunday I _____ a lot because my house was a mess.

3 Yesterday was a lovely day so I _____ for a walk in the park.

4 I usually walk, but yesterday I _____ to work by bus.

5 On Saturday night we _____ to the beach. We _____ a really good time.

6 I _____ my homework on the bus this morning.

7 The party wasn't very good so we _____ home early.

🔊 **9.15** Listen and check.

Talking about you

5 Complete the sentences with what *you* did.

1 Yesterday I **had** a shower at _____ o'clock.

2 This morning I _____ breakfast at _____ o'clock.

3 Last Saturday I _____ shopping, and I bought _____ .

4 Last weekend I _____ my homework at _____ o'clock on _____ .

5 Last year I _____ on holiday to _____ .

6 Tell a partner what you did.

⟩ Go online for more **vocabulary** practice

Everyday English

When's your birthday?

1 These are the months of the year. What is the correct order?

January
_____
_____
_____
_____
_____
_____
_____
_____
_____
_____
_____

🔊 **9.16** Listen and check. Say the months around the class.

2 Which month is your birthday? Tell the class.

> My birthday's in September.

> So is my birthday!

How many birthdays are in each month? Which month has the most birthdays?

3 🔊 **9.17** Listen and repeat the numbers.

first (**1st**)	second (**2nd**)	third (**3rd**)
fourth (**4th**)	fifth (**5th**)	sixth (**6th**)
seventh (**7th**)	eighth (**8th**)	ninth (**9th**)
tenth (**10th**)	eleventh (**11th**)	twelfth (**12th**)
thirteenth (**13th**)	fourteenth (**14th**)	fifteenth (**15th**)

4 Say these numbers.

16th	17th	18th	19th	20th	21st	22nd	23rd
24th	25th	26th	27th	28th	29th	30th	31st

🔊 **9.18** Listen and check.

5 🔊 **9.19** Listen and write the numbers. Practise them.

the _____ of January
the _____ of March
the _____ of May
the _____ of June
the _____ of November
the _____ of December

> **❗ TIP**
>
> **We say:**
> the tenth of April
> **We write:**
> 10 April   April 10   10/4/17
> **Americans write:**
> 4/10/17

6 When is your birthday? Do you know what time you were born? Ask and answer in groups.

> When's your birthday?

> It's on the third of March.

> What time were you born?

> At two o'clock in the morning.

Tell the class.

> I was born in 1996 on the twentieth of July at two o'clock in the morning.

7 🔊 **9.20** It's Sarah's birthday. Listen to the song. Sing _Happy Birthday!_ to Sarah.

🔗 Go online for more **speaking** practice

Grammar reference

➔ 9.1 *was/were*

Was and *were* are the past tense of *am/are/is.*

Present

I	am	
He/She It	is	fine. in class.
You We They	are	

Past

I He/She It	was	fine.
You We They	were	at home.

Negative

I He	wasn't	at home last weekend. at school yesterday.
You They	weren't	

Questions

Where **were you** yesterday?
Was she at school?   Yes, **she was.**/No, **she wasn't**.

❶ We use *was/were* with *born*, not *am/is/are*.

Where **were** you **born**?	NOT	~~Where are you born?~~
He **was born** in Russia.		~~He is born in Russia.~~

➔ 9.2 Past Simple – irregular verbs

Many common verbs are irregular. See the list of irregular verbs on the inside front cover.

Present	→	Past
am/is/are		was/were
buy		bought
do		did
go		went
have		had
make		made
put		put
run		ran
see		saw
sit		sat

Wordlist

adj = adjective	n = noun	pron = pronoun
adv = adverb	pl = plural	v = verb
conj = conjunction	prep = preposition	infml = informal

amazed   *adj* /ə'meɪzd/   _____
angry   *adj* /'æŋgri/   _____
astronaut   *n* /'æstrənɔːt/   _____
birthday   *n* /'bɜːθdeɪ/   _____
born   *v* /bɔːn/   _____
boxer   *n* /'bɒksə(r)/   _____
check   *v* /tʃek/   _____
explorer   *n* /ɪk'splɔːrə(r)/   _____
find   *v* /faɪnd/   _____
grandmother   *n* /'grænmʌðə(r)/   _____
grandson   *n* /'grænsʌn/   _____
housework   *n* /'haʊswɜːk/   _____
inventor   *n* /ɪn'ventə(r)/   _____
jackpot   *n* /'dʒækpɒt/   _____
last year   /ˌlɑːst 'jɪə(r)/   _____
lottery   *n* /'lɒtəri/   _____
make   *v* /meɪk/   _____
million   *n* /'mɪljən/   _____
newsagent's   *n* /'njuːzeɪdʒənts/   _____
pocket   *n* /'pɒkɪt/   _____
politician   *n* /ˌpɒlə'tɪʃn/   _____
princess   *n* /ˌprɪn'ses/   _____
put   *v* /pʊt/   _____
run   *v* /rʌn/   _____
scientist   *n* /'saɪəntɪst/   _____
see   *v* /siː/   _____
singer   *n* /'sɪŋə(r)/   _____
sit   *v* /sɪt/   _____
story   *n* /'stɔːri/   _____
thousand   *n* /'θaʊzənd/   _____
washing machine   *n* /'wɒʃɪŋ məˌʃiːn/_____
writer   *n* /'raɪtə(r)/   _____
yesterday   *adv* /'jestədeɪ/   _____

Months of the year
January   *n* /'dʒænjuəri/   _____
February   *n* /'februəri/   _____
March   *n* /mɑːtʃ/   _____
April   *n* /'eɪprəl/   _____
May   *n* /meɪ/   _____
June   *n* /dʒuːn/   _____
July   *n* /dʒu'laɪ/   _____
August   *n* /'ɔːgəst/   _____
September   *n* /sep'tembə(r)/   _____
October   *n* /ɒk'təʊbə(r)/   _____
November   *n* /nəʊ'vembə(r)/   _____
December   *n* /dɪ'sembə(r)/   _____

Ordinal numbers
first   /fɜːst/   _____
second   /'sekənd/   _____
third   /θɜːd/   _____
fourth   /fɔːθ/   _____
fifth   /fɪfθ/   _____
sixth   /sɪksθ/   _____
seventh   /'sevnθ/   _____
eighth   /eɪtθ/   _____
ninth   /naɪnθ/   _____
tenth   /tenθ/   _____

We had a good time!

- Grammar **Past Simple – regular and irregular verbs**
- Vocabulary **Sport and leisure**
- Everyday English **Going sightseeing**
- Listening **Gary and Cathy's holidays**
- Speaking **Making conversation**
- Writing **My last holiday**

Work with a partner. Answer the questions.

1 What day is it today? What day was it yesterday? What day is it tomorrow?

2 Where were you yesterday?

A holiday selfie in front of the Brandenburg Gate, Germany

 Watch the video introduction online

 Use your **Workbook** for self study

 **Go online** for more practice and to *Check your Progress*

Yesterday was Sunday

1 Match a sentence with a time expression.

We're at home	in 2015.
I went to Australia	at 5p.m.
I bought a nice dress	yesterday.
They weren't at school	now.

2 What is the past tense of these irregular verbs?

buy	go	do
get	have	leave
meet	see	take

Grammar

Past Simple – regular and irregular verbs

1 🔊 **10.1** Listen to Kristin. Tick (✓) the things she did yesterday.

Yesterday she ...

- [ ] **got up** early
- [ ] **had** breakfast in bed
- [ ] **saw** her grandmother
- [ ] **listened** to music
- [ ] **called** a friend
- [ ] **went** running
- [ ] **met** some friends

- [ ] **bought** some bread
- [ ] **invited** friends to her flat
- [ ] **cooked** a meal
- [ ] **played** cards
- [ ] **watched** a film
- [ ] **cleaned** her flat
- [ ] **did** some work at her desk

● GRAMMAR SPOT

1 Underline the irregular verbs in the list in exercise **1**.

2 The other verbs are regular. What are the last two letters? Write the Past Simple forms of these verbs.

/t/	cook	_cooked_	watch	_____
/d/	play	_____	listen	_____
/ɪd/	start	_____	invite	_____

🔊 **10.2** Listen and repeat.

3 The Past Simple is the same for *I/you/he/she/it/ we/they*.

| I/you/he/she/it/we/they | played |
| | went |

→ Grammar reference 10.1 ▷ p100

2 Tell the class what Kristin did.

> Yesterday she got up late and had ... . Then she ... .

3 What did you do last Sunday? Look at the list in exercise 1 and tell a partner.

> Last Sunday I got up ... and I went ... I saw ...

Past Simple – questions and negatives

Monday morning

1 🔊 **10.3** It is Monday morning. Kristin and Dave are at work. Listen and complete their conversation.

K Morning, Dave. [1] _**Did**_ you _**have**_ a good weekend?

D Yes, I did, thanks.

K So, what [2]_____ you do yesterday?

D Well, I got up really early, and I [3]_____ golf with some friends.

K You [4]_____ up early on Sunday! Are you crazy!

D Yes, I know, but it was such a lovely day – I didn't want to stay in bed – and I love playing golf.

K Mmm, I love my bed, not golf! Where [5]_____ you _____?

D At my local golf club. After we finished our game, we [6]_____ lunch in the clubhouse. The food is really good there.

K Great! [7]_____ you _____ out in the evening?

D No, I didn't go out – I was too tired. My sister visited me, and she [8]_____ dinner for me. She's a great cook.

K Lucky you! What [9]_____ you _____?

D Lasagne. It was delicious. What about you, Kristin? Did _you_ have a good weekend?

● **GRAMMAR SPOT**

Present Simple questions and negatives

1 Questions and negatives use **do** and **does**.
   Do you **like** golf? No, I **don't**.
   Does she **like** golf? No, she **doesn't**.

Past Simple questions and negatives

2 All questions use **did**. Complete the questions.
   **Did** she **have** a good weekend?   Where _____ they **play**?
   What _**did**_ you **do** yesterday?   When _____ you **go**?
   🔊 **10.4** Listen and repeat.

3 All negatives use **didn't**. Complete the negatives.
   He _**didn't want**_ to stay in bed.
   They _____ **go out**.   I _____ **cook** a meal.
   🔊 **10.5** Listen and repeat.

➔ Grammar reference 10.2   ▷ p100

2 Work with a partner. Practise the conversation in exercise 1.

3 🔊 **10.6** Listen to Dave asking Kristin about _her_ weekend. Complete the questions.

   1 What / do on Saturday?
     What did you do on Saturday?
   2 Who / see at the party?
   3 … get home / late?
   4 What / do / after breakfast on Sunday?
   5 What / do in the afternoon?
   6 … do anything / Sunday evening?

4 Ask and answer the questions about Kristin with your partner.

   What did Kristin do on Saturday?

5 Say some things Kristin and Dave _didn't_ do.

   Kristin:
   • big breakfast
   • her grandmother
   • cards

   Dave:
   • late
   • shopping
   • a party

   Kristin didn't have a big breakfast.
   Dave didn't get up late.

Talking about you

6 Work with a partner. Say what you did and didn't do yesterday evening.

   What did you do yesterday evening?

   I didn't do much. I stayed at home.

   ▶ **Go online** to **watch** a video where people talk about what they did at the weekend.

Practice

Did you have a good weekend?

1 What activities are in the photos?

2 Look at the questionnaire. Put a tick (✓) next to the things *you* did last weekend.

3 Ask your teacher the questions. Put a tick (✓) next to the things he/she did.

> Did you cook dinner?
>
> Yes, I did./No, I didn't.

4 Ask a partner the questions. Put a tick (✓) next to the things he/she did.

Tell the class about your partner.

> Peter played football and he did a lot of housework. He didn't go to a party, but he went shopping.

Time expressions

5 Complete the time expressions using a word from the box.

| at | in | on | last | yesterday |

on	Wednesday
_____	8 o'clock
_____	the morning
_____	week
_____	2017
I went there … _____	month
_____	June 3rd
_____	the weekend
_____	Monday morning
_____	evening

🔊 10.7 Listen and check.

Questionnaire
LAST WEEKEND

Did you …?	You	Teacher	Partner
go to the cinema	☐	☐	☐
go shopping	☐	☐	☐
cook dinner	☐	☐	☐
watch TV	☐	☐	☐
play football	☐	☐	☐
go to a party	☐	☐	☐
see your friends	☐	☐	☐
have coffee in a coffee shop	☐	☐	☐
do a lot of housework	☐	☐	☐
do a lot of homework	☐	☐	☐

6 Complete the sentences with a verb in the Past Simple and a word from exercise 5.

1 She **_started_** (start) doing her homework **at** 5 o'clock and she _____ (not finish) until bedtime.

2 I _____ (not play) golf [____] the weekend.

3 'What _____ you _____ (do) [____] the evening?'
'We _____ (have) dinner with friends.'

4 We _____ (go) to the cinema [____] Saturday afternoon.

5 'When _____ you _____ (work) in New York?'
'[____] 2015, for six months.'

6 'When is Ted's birthday?'
'It was [____] September 17th. I _____ (buy) him a jumper.'

Check it

7 Tick (✓) the correct sentence.

1 ☐ They left the party early.
☐ They leaved the party early.

2 ☐ Did you go skiing in January?
☐ Did you go skiing at January?

3 ☐ Did they went shopping yesterday?
☐ Did they go shopping yesterday?

4 ☐ What did you do last weekend?
☐ What did you last weekend?

5 ☐ 'Did you like the film?' 'Yes, I did.'
☐ 'Did you like the film?' 'Yes, I liked.'

6 ☐ I saw John on last night.
☐ I saw John last night.

▶ Go online for more **grammar** practice

Speaking
Making conversation

1 In conversation, we ask questions to show we are interested.

> We went to the cinema last night.

> Oh, really? What did you see?

> Was it good?   Who was in it?

Reply to these lines with a question.

1 'I went shopping yesterday.'
'Really? (Where/go?) *Where did you go?*'

2 'We went to that new Italian restaurant last night.'
'Mmm! (What/have?) _____?'

3 'We saw a lot of our friends in the coffee shop.'
'Oh! (Who/see?) _____?'

4 'I played tennis at the weekend.'
'Oh, really? (Where/play?) _____?'

5 'The party on Saturday was great!'
'Oh, good! (What time/leave?) _____?'

🔊 **10.8** Listen and check.

2 Work with a partner. Read the example conversation.

A I went shopping yesterday.
B Really? Where did you go?
A Oxford Street.
B Oh, lovely! What did you buy?
A Well, I wanted a new dress for a friend's wedding, and I went to Selfridges.
B Selfridges? Nice, but expensive! Did you find one?
A Yes, I did. I found a beautiful blue one in the sale. It was only £65!
B Wow! Well done!

Choose one of the conversations in exercise 1 and make it longer.

🔊 **10.9** Listen and compare.

Vocabulary and speaking
Sport and leisure

1 What are the activities in the photos?

3 rugby		☐ sailing	
☐ skiing		☐ tennis	
☐ ice-skating		☐ canoeing	
☐ cycling		☐ cards	
☐ golf		☐ running	
☐ walking		☐ swimming	
☐ fishing		☐ volleyball	
☐ windsurfing			

2 Write the activities in the correct column.

play	go + -ing
rugby	*skiing*

Talking about you

3 Work with a partner. Ask and answer questions about the activities.

> **Do you play tennis?**
> **Yes, I do.**

> **When did you last play?**
> **Last week.**

> **Do you go skiing?**
> **No, I don't.**

4 Tell the class about your partner.

> **Gina doesn't play golf, but she goes cycling. Last year she went cycling in France.**

↪ Go online for more **vocabulary** practice

Listening and speaking
Gary and Cathy's holidays

1 Say the months of the year.

> January February …

In your country, what months are …?

> spring summer autumn winter

2 When do you usually go on holiday? Where do you usually go on holiday?

> I usually go on holiday in summer.

> I usually go to Spain.

3 ◀)) 10.10 Listen to Cathy and Gary talking about their holidays. Underline what they say.

They usually …	But last year they …
1 go in *autumn* / *winter*.	went in *spring* / *summer*.
2 go to *Barbados* / *Dubai*.	went to *Florida* / *France*.
3 go *swimming* / *sailing*.	went *canoeing* / *cycling*.
4 stay in a *villa* / *hotel*.	stayed in a *tent* / *cabin*.
5 eat *in the hotel* / *at expensive restaurants*.	*cooked outside* / *went to cafés*.
6 play *cards* / *golf*.	*went fishing* / *played tennis*.
7 *have* / *don't have* a good time.	*also had* / *didn't have* a good time.

4 Ask and answer questions with a partner about Gary and Cathy's holidays.

1 When / go?
2 Where / go?
3 Where / stay?
4 Where / eat?
5 What / do?
6 … have a good time?

> When do they usually go on holiday?

> In winter.

> When did they go last year?

> In summer.

5 Complete the sentences about Gary and Cathy's last holiday.

Last year…

1 They *didn't go* on holiday in winter, they _____ in summer.
2 They _____ to Barbados, they _____ to the Ardèche, in France.
3 They _____ in a hotel, they _____ in a cabin.
4 They _____ in restaurants, they _____ outside.
5 They _____ swimming, they _____ canoeing.

6 Work with a partner. Which do you think is the best holiday? Why?

Speaking and writing
My last holiday

1 What is your favourite kind of holiday?
What do you like doing? ✓
What don't you like? ✗

- [ ] relaxing on a beach
- [ ] camping by a river
- [ ] going skiing
- [ ] walking in the mountains
- [ ] sightseeing in famous cities
- [ ] eating at different restaurants
- [ ] playing sports
- [ ] visiting museums

Compare your choices with a partner.

2 What did you do on your last holiday? Ask and answer questions with a partner.

- Where … go?
- When … go?
- Where … stay?
- What … do every day?
- … you have good weather?
- What … do in the evening?
- What … eat?
- … nice people?

> **Where did you go?**
> **I went to Scotland.**

> **When did you go?**
> **Last year./Two years ago.**

3 Tell the class about your partner.

Karl went sightseeing in Rome last June/six months ago.

> ● **GRAMMAR SPOT**
>
> *ago*
> *Two years ago* means *two years before now*.
> I met James **ten years ago**.
> I went to New York **six weeks ago**.
> Sally phoned **five minutes ago**.
>
> ➔ Grammar reference 10.3 ▷ p100

Writing

4 Write about your last holiday. Read it to the class.

My last holiday

Last …, I went on holiday to … . I went
with … . We stayed in … . Every day we … .
Sometimes we … . Once we … . We met … .
The food was … . and the weather was … .
We had a … time.

📲 Go online for more **writing** practice

Everyday English
Going sightseeing

1 Write the names of two cities and the dates when you were a tourist there.

Paris, July 2010   Istanbul, April 2014

Show a partner. Talk about the cities.

What did you do there? What did you see there? What did you buy?

 I went to … We visited …

 We saw … I bought …

2 🔊 **10.11** Listen and complete the conversations in a tourist office.

1 **A** Hello. Can I ¹_____ _____?

    B Yes. ²_____ _____ have a map of the city, please?

    A Of course. Here you are.

    B Can you show ³_____ where we are on the ⁴_____?

    A Yes. We're ⁵_____ in Regent Street in the city ⁶_____.

2 **C** We want to go on a ¹_____ tour of the ²_____.

    A That's fine. The next bus ³_____ at 10 o'clock. It ⁴_____ about an hour and a half.

    C Where does the bus go from?

    A It ⁵_____ _____ Trafalgar Square, but you can get ⁶_____ and off when you want.

3 **D** I want to visit the British Museum. What time does it ¹_____?

    A It opens at 10 in the morning and ²_____ at 5.30 in the evening.

    D ³_____ _____ is it to get in?

    A It's ⁴_____!

Work with a partner. Practise the conversations.

3 When people go sightseeing in your town, where do they go? What is there to do in your town?

We have a beautiful cathedral.   There's a park and a zoo.

Visitors go to the market/the old town/the square …

Roleplay

4 Roleplay a conversation in a tourist office with your partner.

Student A
You are a tourist at the tourist office.
Ask for information.

Student B
You work in the tourist office in your home town.
Give information.

🔗 Go online for more **speaking** practice

Grammar reference

→ 10.1 Past Simple positive

1 Regular verbs add -ed in the Past Simple.

Present	→	Past
play		play**ed**
watch		watch**ed**
listen		listen**ed**
clean		clean**ed**
invite		invit**ed**

❶ Remember: Many common verbs are irregular.

go	**went**
see	**saw**
have	**had**

See the list of irregular verbs on the inside front cover.

2 The form is the same for all persons.

I You He/She/It We They	listen**ed** **went** **had**	to music. to work. lunch.

→ 10.2 Past Simple questions and negatives

❶ Present → Past
do/does **did**

*What time **does** he usually **get up**?*

*What time **did** he **get up** yesterday?*

Questions with question words

Where	**did**	I you he/she/it we they	**go?**

Negative

I You He/She/It We They	**didn't**	**go** shopping. **see** the film.

Yes/No questions and short answers

Did they **play** football?	Yes, they **did**.
Did you **have** a good time?	No, I **didn't**.

→ 10.3 Past time expressions

I went to London	**three years ago.** **last year.** **yesterday.** **in 2016.**

PAST ← → PRESENT

April   May   June   July

a month ago

two months ago

three months ago

Wordlist

adj = adjective	*excl* = exclamation	*prep* = preposition
adv = adverb	*n* = noun	*pron* = pronoun
conj = conjunction	*pl* = plural	*v* = verb

ago   *adv* /əˈɡəʊ/   _____

autumn   *n* /ˈɔːtəm/   _____

bedtime   *n* /ˈbedtaɪm/   _____

cabin   *n* /ˈkæbɪn/   _____

call   *v* /kɔːl/   _____

camping   *n* /ˈkæmpɪŋ/   _____

canoeing   *n* /kəˈnuːɪŋ/   _____

cards   *n pl* /ˌkɑːdz/   _____

castle   *n* /ˈkɑːsl/   _____

cathedral   *n* /kəˈθiːdrəl/   _____

choose   *v* /tʃuːz/   _____

clean   *v* /kliːn/   _____

clubhouse   *n* /ˈklʌbhaʊs/   _____

coffee shop   *n* /ˈkɒfi ˌʃɒp/   _____

crazy   *adj* /ˈkreɪzi/   _____

cycling   *n* /ˈsaɪklɪŋ/   _____

dancing   *n* /ˈdɑːnsɪŋ/   _____

date   *n* /deɪt/   _____

dress   *n* /dres/   _____

fishing   *n* /ˈfɪʃɪŋ/   _____

ice-skating   *n* /ˈaɪs ˌskeɪtɪŋ/   _____

interested   *n* /ˈɪntrəstɪd/   _____

invite   *v* /ɪnˈvaɪt/   _____

leisure   *n* /ˈleʒə(r)/   _____

lucky   *adj* /ˈlʌki/   _____

market   *n* /ˈmɑːkɪt/   _____

meal   *n* /miːl/   _____

museum   *n* /mjuˈziːəm/   _____

once   *adv* /wʌns/   _____

orange juice   *n* /ˈɒrɪndʒ ˌdʒuːs/   _____

outside   *adv* /ˌaʊtˈsaɪd/   _____

rain   *v* /reɪn/   _____

Really?   *excl* /ˈriːəli/   _____

relax   *v* /rɪˈlæks/   _____

rugby   *n* /ˈrʌɡbi/   _____

sailing   *n* /ˈseɪlɪŋ/   _____

show   *v* /ʃəʊ/   _____

sightseeing   *n* /ˈsaɪtsiːɪŋ/   _____

skiing   *n* /skiːɪŋ/   _____

spring   *n* /sprɪŋ/   _____

start   *v* /stɑːt/   _____

summer   *n* /ˈsʌmə(r)/   _____

tent   *n* /tent/   _____

tour   *n* /tʊə(r)/   _____

tourist   *n* /ˈtʊərɪst/   _____

tourist office   *n* /ˈtʊərɪst ˌɒfɪs/   _____

villa   *n* /ˈvɪlə/   _____

volleyball   *n* /ˈvɒlibɔːl/   _____

walking   *n* /ˈwɔːkɪŋ/   _____

wedding   *n* /ˈwedɪŋ/   _____

windsurfing   *n* /ˈwɪndsɜːfɪŋ/   _____

winter   *n* /ˈwɪntə(r)/   _____

zoo   *n* /zuː/   _____

We can do it! 11

- Grammar **can/can't; Adverbs of manner**
- Vocabulary **Adjective + noun (2)**
- Everyday English **Everyday problems**

- Reading **The Smartphone**
- Listening **What can you do on your smartphone?**

1 What are you good at? Tick (✓).
- [ ] singing
- [ ] making cakes
- [ ] dancing
- [ ] swimming
- [ ] playing computer games
- [ ] playing a musical instrument

2 Work with a partner. Talk about what you are and aren't good at.
I'm good at dancing, but I'm not good at …

3 Find two activities you're both good at.
We're both good at dancing.

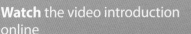 **Watch** the video introduction online

 Use your **Workbook** for self study

Go online for more practice and to *Check your Progress*

What can they do?

Match the words and the photos.

| athlete   dad   pilot   schoolgirl   ~~interpreter~~   musician   mechanic |

1 *interpreter*

2

3

4

5

6

7

Grammar
can/can't

1 Complete the sentences with a word from the Starter.

1 Marcus is a/an *interpreter* . He can speak German and Spanish fluently.
2 Seb is a/an _____ . He can run very fast.
3 Tomas is a/an _____ . He can mend cars.
4 Anna is a/an _____ . She can fly an Airbus A380.
5 Sara is a/an _____ . She can play the violin really well.
6 Lucy is a/an _____ . She can write interesting stories.
7 Leo is Lucy's _____ . He can make fantastic cakes.

🔊 **11.1** Listen and check. Practise the sentences.

2 Tell your partner what you can do from exercise 1.

> I can run fast and I can speak German.

Questions and negatives

1 🔊 11.2 Listen and repeat the questions and answers.

Can Marcus **speak** Spanish?   Yes, he **can**.
Can you **speak** Spanish?   No, I **can't**.
Can Leo **make** cakes?   Yes, he **can**.
Can you **make** cakes?   No, I **can't**. I can't cook at all!

2 Ask and answer questions with a partner. First ask about the people on page 102, then ask about your partner.

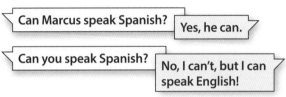

Can Marcus speak Spanish? — Yes, he can.

Can you speak Spanish? — No, I can't, but I can speak English!

Of course I can!

3 🔊 11.4 Read and listen to Lucy and her grandad, James. Complete the conversation.

4 Answer the questions about Lucy.

1 What can Lucy do? What can't she do?
2 What is her favourite game?
3 Who can speak French well?
4 What language can Lucy's grandad speak?
5 What did Lucy do yesterday?

● **GRAMMAR SPOT**

1 *Can/Can't* have the same form for all persons.

I / You / He / She / It / We / They	can can't	speak French.

2 🔊 11.3 Listen to the different pronunciations of *can* and *can't* and repeat.

/kən/
He can make cakes.

/kɑːnt/
He can't run fast.

/kən/
A Can you cook?

/kæn/
B Yes, I can.

➔ **Grammar reference 11.1** ▸ **p110**

James Lucy, you're really good at using the computer. I can't do that. Can you do lots of things on it?

Lucy Of course I ¹_____, Grandad! I can play lots of games on it. My favourite game is *Minecraft* – you can build your own house. It's great!

J Wow! Can you build a house for me?

L Of course I can. I ²_____ make a really big one for you with six bedrooms.

J Six bedrooms – amazing! What other things can you ³_____ on your computer?

L Lots and lots. I can do my maths homework and write stories. Sometimes I ⁴_____ my stories to my friends, and I can chat to my friends, too.

J Wow! That is clever. Now, your mum says you ⁵_____ speak a little French?

L Don't tell Mum, but I'm terrible at French. I ⁶_____ speak it at all. But my friend Helen can speak French really well because her mum's French. They ⁷_____ French at home all the time.

J Well, you can learn from Helen. ⁸_____ you speak any other languages?

L No, I ⁹_____. Can you speak French, Grandad?

J No, I can't, but I can speak German. What other things can you do?

L I can cook! I can ¹⁰_____ delicious cakes! Dad makes great cakes, and sometimes I help him. Yesterday we made a really big chocolate cake!

J Mmm! Can I have some?

L Of course you can.

▶ **Go online** to **watch** a video about a craft show.

Practice

He can speak Portuguese very well!

1 🔊 **11.5** Bobby Boyd is Irish, but he lives in Lisbon, in Portugal. Listen and tick (✓) the things he can do.

Can Bobby … ?

1 ☐ speak Portuguese		5 ☐ sing Fado	
2 ☐ speak German		6 ☐ play the guitar	
3 ☐ ride a horse		7 ☐ cook sardines	
4 ☐ surf		8 ☐ make Irish coffee	

2 Complete Bobby's sentences with words from the box.

> a little bit   fluently   quite well   really well
> (not) at all   very well

1 I can speak Portuguese _____ .

2 I can speak German _____ .

3 All my Portuguese friends can surf _____ .

4 I can't surf _____ .

5 I can sing Fado _____ .

6 I can't cook _____ .

🔊 **11.5** Listen again and practise the sentences.

Pronunciation

3 🔊 **11.6** Listen and <u>underline</u> *can* or *can't*.

1 I *can* / *can't* ski quite well.

2 She *can* / *can't* speak German at all.

3 He *can* / *can't* speak English fluently.

4 Why *can* / *can't* you come to my party?

5 We *can* / *can't* run fast.

6 They *can* / *can't* read music.

7 *Can* / *Can't* you play the violin?

8 *Can* / *Can't* cats swim?

🔊 **11.6** Listen again and repeat.

● **GRAMMAR SPOT**

1 Adverbs can come after the verb.

   They can run **fast**.
   He plays football **well**.

2 Regular adverbs end in **-ly**.

   She can speak French **fluently**.
   Please speak more **slowly**.

➔ Grammar reference 11.2 ▶ p110

Talking about you

4 Complete the chart about you. Then ask and answer the questions with another student.

> **Can you speak German?** **A little bit. Can you?**

> **No, I can't speak German at all.**

Can … ?	You	_____
speak German	☐	☐
ride a horse	☐	☐
surf	☐	☐
play the guitar	☐	☐
dance	☐	☐
cook	☐	☐
drive	☐	☐
swim	☐	☐

5 Compare yourself with other students.

> **Dominic and I can cook very well. He can sing, too, but I can't sing at all.**

Grammar
Requests and offers

1 Look at the pictures. Use the words to write questions with *Can …?*

help Can you I ?

1 *Can I help you?*

time me tell Can you the ?

2

lift a you give Can I ?

3

the have I Can please bill ?

4

slowly more you ? speak please Can

5

for me Can the please ? open you door

6

2 Match these answers with the questions in exercise 1.

a ___3___ Yes, please! That's so kind of you!
b _____ I'm sorry. Is this better? Can you understand me now?
c _____ Yes. Can you tell us about this TV, please?
d _____ Of course I can. Careful!
e _____ It's 4 o'clock.
f _____ Yes, of course. Here you are.

🔊 11.7 Listen and check.

3 Practise the questions and answers with a partner. Continue the conversations.

> Can I give you a lift?
> Oh yes please! That's so kind of you!

> Where do you want to go?
> To the station, please.

Check it

4 Tick (✓) the correct sentence.

1 ☐ I no can understand.
  ☐ I can't understand.

2 ☐ He can drive fast cars.
  ☐ He cans drive fast cars.

3 ☐ Can you swim fast?
  ☐ Do you can swim fast?

4 ☐ We can to play tennis quite well.
  ☐ We can play tennis quite well.

5 ☐ You speak Spanish very good.
  ☐ You speak Spanish very well.

6 ☐ He plays very well the piano.
  ☐ He plays the piano very well.

↪ Go online for more **grammar** practice

Reading and speaking
The Smartphone

1 Look at these apps. What are they for?

1  2   3

4  5  6

2 Match the verbs and nouns.

Verbs	Nouns
send	a friend
play	a bill
text	a message
take	games
pay	photos

Verbs	Nouns
listen	a hotel
watch	videos
read	information on the Internet
book	emails
find	to music

Which of these things do you do on your phone?

I send messages. I read emails.

3 What do you know about smartphones? Discuss the questions.
- When did we start to use smartphones?
- Why do we use smartphones so much?

4 🔊 11.8 Read and listen to the text about smartphones. Answer the questions in exercise 3.

5 All the sentences below are false. Read the text again and correct them.
1 Apple made the first smartphone.
2 The first smartphone was cheap.
3 Only a few people used Blackberries.
4 A satnav app can drive your car.
5 Our phones can sing songs for us.

What can't you do on your SMARTPHONE?

The history

Was there ever a world with no smartphones? Well, yes there was! IBM made the first smartphone in 1993. It was big and heavy. It also cost an amazing $899! The first Blackberry went on sale in 2002. Tens of millions of people used the Blackberry. It sent emails and 'surfed' the net. In 2007 Apple's first iPhone arrived in the shops and it was very popular. Today Samsung sells the most smartphones worldwide.

The first smartphone

Now more people in the world have mobile phones than have toilets, and we use our smartphones more than 110 times a day!

NOT MUCH!

Hundreds of uses

Of course, you **can text** friends, send emails and take photos and videos with your phone, but we use our phones for so much more. Our phones **can open** and lock our front doors, and a satnav app **can give** us directions when we're lost! There's an app that tells us how healthy we are and there's even an app that tells us how well we sleep. We **can ask** our phone what song is on the radio, we **can play** chess with a friend thousands of miles away and we **can Skype** our family when we're not at home. The smartphone is a really important part of our lives.

> We can't live without it!

Listening and speaking
What do you do on your smartphone?

1 Work with a partner. Look at the photos. These people use their phones a lot. Who do you think says the lines below?

1 I often go on Facebook too – it's a great way to get everybody's news and we can share all our photos.
2 Mostly I play games on it with my friends. My favourite game is *Flappy Birds*.
3 I live in Scotland and my son lives in London. Playing *Scrabble* makes us feel nearby.
4 It is amazing that I can send a video from Mumbai in India and it's on the 6 o'clock news!
5 I use *FaceTime* to see and speak to my family so I don't feel so sad. I can even see my dog, Clara.
6 I can arrange meetings and talk to clients when I'm on the train.

1 KEITH, 73

2 MADDIE, 34

3 ANTONIO, 21

4 KYLIE, 17

5 JOSH, 8

6 TAYLOR, 42

🔊 **11.9** Listen and check your ideas. Were you right?

2 🔊 **11.9** Listen to the people again. When do they use their phones? What other information do you learn about each person?

What do you think?
- Which of the six people do you think most needs their phone?
- Can you live without your phone?
- What are the most important things you use your phone for?
- What are your favourite apps/games?

Vocabulary and speaking
Adjective + noun (2)

1 Work with a partner. Match the groups of adjectives with the noun.

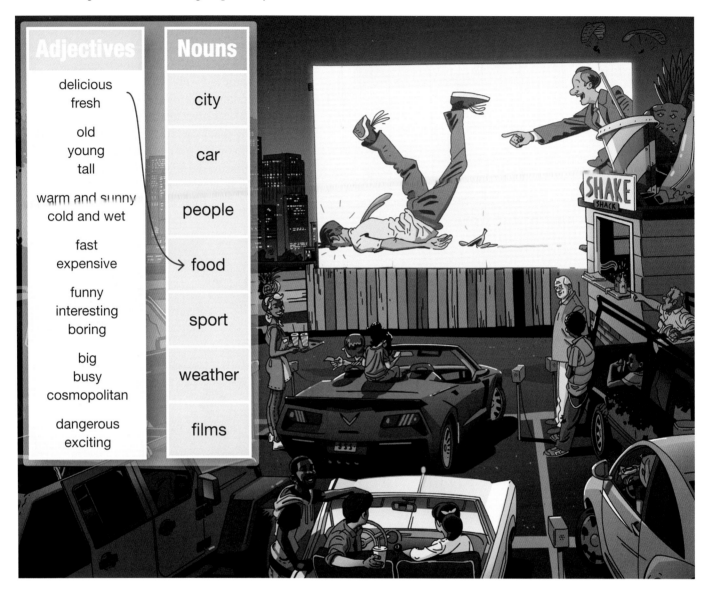

Adjectives	Nouns
delicious fresh	city
old young tall	car
warm and sunny cold and wet	people
fast expensive	food
funny interesting boring	sport
big busy cosmopolitan	weather
dangerous exciting	films

2 Complete the sentences with words from exercise 1. Compare answers with a partner.

1 A Ferrari is an *expensive car*.
2 We can't go for a walk, it's too *cold and wet*.
3 'How _____ is your brother?'
   'He's very _____, 1.9 metres.'
4 I think motor racing is a _____.
5 Can I have a _____ orange juice, please?
6 New York is a very _____.
7 Charlie Chaplin made some very _____.

🔊 11.10 Listen and compare. Look at audioscript 11.10 on page 144 and practise the conversations.

3 Work in groups. Think of examples of these things.

an **expensive car** and a **cheap car**

a **dangerous sport** and a **safe sport**

an **old city** and a **modern city**

an **old film star** and a **young film star**

a **funny film** and a **boring film**

Compare your lists.

⤴ **Go online** for more **vocabulary** practice

Everyday English

Everyday problems

1 Match the photos to the problems.

6	computers		arriving late
	directions		a ticket machine
	lost keys		an accident

2 Match the lines with the photos.

4	*I can't find them anywhere!*
	This machine doesn't work.
	I'm lost!
	I'm so sorry I'm late!
	I can't get on the Internet!
	Are you all right?

3 🔊 11.11 Listen and complete the conversations.

1
> **A** Excuse me! Can you help me? I'm lost.
> **B** Where do you ¹_____ to go?
> **A** The Canadian Embassy.
> **B** Turn left onto Trafalgar Square. It's ²_____ on. You ³_____ miss it.

2
> **A** Excuse me! This ticket machine ¹_____.
> **B** Did you ²_____ the green button?
> **A** No, I didn't.
> **B** Ah, well. Here's your ³_____ .
> **A** Thank you very much.

3
> **A** I'm so sorry ¹_____ .
> **B** It's OK. The film ²_____ in 15 minutes!
> **A** I missed the ³_____ .
> **B** I told you, it doesn't ⁴_____ . Come on! Let's go.

4
> **A** Come on! It's time to leave.
> **B** But I ¹_____ the car keys! I can't find them anywhere!
> **A** You ²_____ them in your bag.
> **B** Did I? Oh yes. ³_____ they are! Phew!

5
> **A** Are you ¹_____ ?
> **B** Yes, I think so.
> **A** Does your arm hurt?
> **B** It hurts ²_____ , but I think it's OK.

6
> **A** Oh no!
> **B** What's the matter?
> **A** There's something ¹_____ with my computer. I can't ²_____ the Internet, so I can't send emails.
> **B** Turn everything off and try ³_____ . That sometimes ⁴_____ .

🔊 11.11 Listen and check. Practise the conversations.

4 Learn two conversations and act them out to the class.

⬀ Go online for more **speaking** practice

Grammar reference

→ 11.1 *can*

Positive

I You He/She/It We They	**can**	swim. drive. cook. run fast.

Negative

I You He/She/It We They	**can't**	draw. speak German. play golf.

Questions with question words

What		you do?
When	**can**	I go home?
How many languages		he speak?

Yes/No questions and short answers

Can you swim?	Yes, I **can**.
Can he play tennis?	No, he **can't**.

We don't use *do/does/don't/doesn't* with *can*.

I can't swim.	NOT	~~I don't can swim.~~
Can you cook?	NOT	~~Do you can cook?~~
She can't speak Spanish.	NOT	~~She doesn't can …~~
They can't dance.	NOT	~~They don't can …~~

→ 11.2 Adverbs

1 Adverbs give more information about verbs.

   go **fast**   draw **well**   sing **beautifully**

2 Notice the word order.

You **speak** *English* **well**.	NOT	~~You speak well English.~~
He **drives** *his car* **fast**.	NOT	~~He drives fast his car.~~

3 Regular adverbs end in *-ly*.

Adjective	→	Adverb
fluent		*fluent**ly***
beautiful		*beautiful**ly***
slow		*slow**ly***
careful		*careful**ly***
usual		*usual**ly***

4 Some adverbs are irregular.

Adjective	→	Adverb
good		**well**
fast		**fast**
late		**late**
early		**early**
hard		**hard**

Wordlist

adj = adjective	*n* = noun *pl* = plural
adv = adverb	*phr* = phrase *pron* = pronoun
conj = conjunction	*phr v* = phrasal verb *v* = verb

accident *n* /'æksɪdənt/	_____
arm *n* /ɑːm/	_____
arrive *v* /ə'raɪv/	_____
athlete *n* /'æθliːt/	_____
bill *n* /bɪl/	_____
button *n* /'bʌtn/	_____
cake *n* /keɪk/	_____
chat *v* /tʃæt/	_____
chess *n* /tʃes/	_____
clever *adj* /'klevə(r)/	_____
cost *v* /kɒst/	_____
dangerous *adj* /'deɪndʒərəs/	_____
everything *pron* /'evriθɪŋ/	_____
fluently *adv* /'fluːəntli/	_____
fly *v* /flaɪ/	_____
get on (the Internet) *phr* /get ɒn (ði 'ɪntənet)/	_____
good at *phr* /'gʊd æt/	_____
grandad *n* /'grændæd/	_____
green *adj* /griːn/	_____
guitar *n* /gɪ'tɑː(r)/	_____
heavy *adj* /'hevi/	_____
help *v* /help/	_____
horse *n* /hɔːs/	_____
hurt *v* /hɜːt/	_____
interpreter *n* /ɪn'tɜːprɪtə(r)/	_____
kind *adj* /kaɪnd/	_____
lift *n* /lɪft/	_____
lock *v* /lɒk/	_____
lost *adj* /lɒst/	_____
mechanic *n* /mə'kænɪk/	_____
mend *v* /mend/	_____
message *n* /'mesɪdʒ/	_____
metre *n* /'miːtə/	_____
mile *n* /maɪl/	_____
miss *v* /mɪs/	_____
pay *v* /peɪ/	_____
pilot *n* /'paɪlət/	_____
popular *adj* /'pɒpjələ(r)/	_____
really well *phr* /,riːəli 'wel/	_____
ride *v* /raɪd/	_____
safe *adj* /seɪf/	_____
satnav *n* /'sætnæv/	_____
send *v* /send/	_____
slowly *adv* /'sləʊli/	_____
something *pron* /'sʌmθɪŋ/	_____
smartphone *n* /'smɑːtfəʊn/	_____
surf *v* /sɜːf/	_____
take photos *phr* /,teɪk 'fəʊtəʊz/	_____
terrible *adj* /'terəbl/	_____
ticket machine *n* /'tɪkɪt mə,ʃiːn/	_____
try *v* /traɪ/	_____
turn off *phr v* /,tɜːn 'ɒf/	_____
violin *n* /,vaɪə'lɪn/	_____
wet *adj* /wet/	_____
What's the matter? /,wɒts ðə 'mætə(r)/	_____
worldwide *adv* /'wɜːldwaɪd/	_____

Thank you very much!

12

- Grammar **I'd like/I'd like to; some/any**
- Vocabulary **In a café**
- Everyday English **Signs all around**
- Listening **Birthday wishes**
- Reading **Meal times around the world**

?

1 What can you buy in a supermarket? Make a list.
milk, ...
2 Work with a partner. Compare your lists.

▶ **Watch** the video introduction online

📄 Use your **Workbook** for self study

↪ **Go online** for more practice and to *Check your Progress*

At the market

1 Match the activities and places. What can you do where?

Activities	Places
1 _g_ buy a magazine	a post office
2 _____ buy aspirin, shampoo …	b bookshop
3 _____ buy stamps and send a parcel	c bank
4 _____ get US dollars	d chemist's
5 _____ buy a dictionary	e supermarket
6 _____ get a medium latte	f coffee shop
7 _____ buy milk, bread, meat, fruit …	g newsagent's

2 Make sentences with *You can …*

You can buy a magazine in a newsagent's.

🔊 **12.1** Listen and check.

Grammar
I'd like/I'd like to; some/any

1 🔊 **12.2** Harry (H) is at the market. Listen and complete the conversations.

1

H Good [1]_____ . I'd like some ham, please.

A How much would you like?

H Hmm. [2]_____ slices.

A Would you like anything else?

H Yes, I'd like some olives. [3]_____ you [4]_____ any green olives?

A I'm afraid I [5]_____ have any green olives. I sold them all. What about black? I have some lovely black olives from Greece.

H OK. Can I have 50 g of black olives? [6]_____ much is that?

2

B Morning, sir. Can I help you?

H Yes, please. I'd like some potatoes.

B Would you [1]_____ some of these? They're very good.

H Yes, please. I'd like a kilo.

B OK. [2]_____ else?

H Er, oh yeah. I don't have any fruit. I'd like [3]_____ oranges, please.

B How [4]_____?

H Six, please.

B Here you are. That's £4.90, please.

🔊 **12.2** Listen again and check. Practise the conversations.

2 **◄))12.3** Harry is still shopping. Listen to his conversations and complete the table.

	Conversation 1	Conversation 2
Where is he now?		
What does he want?		

3 Harry has a visitor, Alice (A). Complete the conversations.

1 H What ¹ *would* you ²_____ _____ drink?

  A A cold drink please. ³_____ you have ⁴_____ apple juice?

  H Er … I have ⁵_____ orange juice, but I don't have ⁶_____ apple juice.

  A Don't worry. Orange juice is fine. Thanks.

2 H ¹_____ you ²_____ something to eat?

  A Yes, please.

  H Is a sandwich OK?

  A A cheese sandwich?

  H Er … I don't have ³_____ cheese. Sorry. I have ⁴_____ ham. What about a ham sandwich?

  A Yes, please.

  H ⁵_____ you ⁶_____ some chocolate cake, too?

  A Yes, please. I'd love some.

◄))12.4 Listen and check. Practise the conversations.

● GRAMMAR SPOT

would like/would like to

1 *I'd like …* is more polite than *I want …*
   I'd like some ham, please.

2 We offer things with *Would you like …?* and *Would you like to…?*
   Would you like anything else?
   Would you like to watch a film?

some and *any*

1 We use *some* in positive sentences.
   I'd like **some** apples.

2 We use *any* with questions and negatives.
   Do you have **any** oranges?
   We don't have **any** oranges.

   We can also use *some* when we offer things.
   Would you like **some** coffee?

➔ Grammar reference 12.1–12.2 ▶ **p120**

Role-play

4 Work with a partner. You have a friend at your house. Offer him/her something to eat or drink.

To drink:	a glass of wine/water a coffee an orange juice
To eat:	a biscuit some cake a sandwich

Would you like a drink? — Yes, please.

What would you like? — A glass of wine, please.

5 Now suggest some things to do.

watch a film	see my holiday photos
sit in the garden	play a computer game
go for a walk	watch the match on TV

Would you like to see my holiday photos? — Yes, I'd love to. Did you have a good time?

▶ Go online to **watch** a video about the Los Angeles food trucks.

Practice

It's my birthday!

1 🔊 **12.5** Listen to the conversation. What does the woman want to do? Why is the man *not* happy?

2 Read and complete the conversation with words from the box.

would you like   I'd like   I'd like to (x3)   some

A Hey, isn't it your birthday soon?

B Yeah, next week on the 15th.

A So, what ¹_____ for your birthday?

B I don't know. I don't need anything.

A But ²_____ buy you something.

B That's kind, but I think ³_____ forget my birthday this year.

A What? You don't want any presents! Why not?

B Well, I'm 30 next week, and that feels old.

A Thirty isn't old. Come on! ⁴_____ take you out for a meal with ⁵_____ friends. You can choose the restaurant.

B OK, then. Thank you. ⁶_____ that. Just don't tell anyone it's my birthday.

A Oh, that's silly!

🔊 **12.5** Listen again and check. Practise the conversations.

Birthday wishes

3 🔊 **12.6** Listen to three people. It's their birthday soon. Complete the chart.

What would they …	… like for a present?	… like to do in the evening?
Jill	*breakfast in bed*	
Sammy		
Zoe		

Talking about you

4 Think about your next birthday. Ask and answer questions about what *you'd* like.

> What would you like for your birthday?

> I'd like a new smartphone and some clothes.

> What would you like to do on your birthday?

> I'd like to go out for a meal with friends.

Grammar

like and *would like*

1 🔊 **12.7** Read and listen to the two conversations. Which conversation is about what you like doing every day? Which is about what you want to do today?

1

> **A** What do you like doing in your free time?
>
> **B** I like playing and watching football, I like going to the cinema and I like watching TV.
>
> **A** What do you like watching?

2

> **A** What would you like to do tonight?
>
> **B** I'd like to go out. What about you?
>
> **A** Good idea! Would you like to go to the cinema?
>
> **B** I'd love to! What's on?
>
> **A** That new film with …

Practise the conversations with a partner.

> ● **GRAMMAR SPOT**
>
> **1** What's the difference between these two sentences?
>
> I **like** Coke.   I**'d like** a Coke.
>
> **2** *Like* refers to **always**.
>
> I **like** coffee.   I **like** going to the cinema.
>
> **3** *'d like* refers to **now** or **soon**.
>
> I**'d like** a coffee, please.   I**'d like to** go to the cinema tonight.
>
> → **Grammar reference 12.3**   ▶ **p120**

Talking about you

2 Work with a partner. Make conversations.

> What do you like doing in your free time?
>
> I like … and I like … What about you?

> What would you like to do this weekend?
>
> Well, I'd like to … What about you?

go for a walk

eat in a restaurant

watch football

make a cake

play tennis

see a film

go shopping

read the newspaper

sleep a lot

go out with friends

Listening and pronunciation

3 🔊 **12.8** Listen to the conversations. Tick (✓) the sentences you hear.

1 ✓ Would you like a Coke?
   ☐ Do you like Coke?

2 ☐ I like watching films.
   ☐ I'd like to watch a film.

3 ☐ We like houses with big kitchens.
   ☐ We'd like a house with a big kitchen.

4 ☐ What would you like to do?
   ☐ What do you like doing?

5 ☐ I like new clothes.
   ☐ I'd like some new clothes.

Look at audioscript 12.8 on page 144 and practise the conversations.

Check it

4 Tick (✓) the correct sentence.

1 ☐ I like leave early today.
   ☐ I'd like to leave early today.

2 ☐ Do you like your job?
   ☐ Would you like your job?

3 ☐ Would you like tea or coffee?
   ☐ You like tea or coffee?

4 ☐ I'd love any cake, please.
   ☐ I'd love some cake, please.

5 ☐ They like something to eat.
   ☐ They'd like something to eat.

6 ☐ I don't need any stamps.
   ☐ I don't need some stamps.

> ⤴ Go online for more **grammar** practice

Reading and speaking
Meal times around the world

1 Match the words and the pictures.

> bread and butter   sausages   chicken   fruit
> fish   rice   vegetables   toast   eggs

2 Work in three groups.

Group A	Read about **Scott Morgan**
Group B	Read about **Min-Jun Gang**
Group C	Read about **Hanna Varga**

Answer the questions.

1 Which food in exercise 1 does he/she eat?
2 What does he/she have for breakfast, lunch and dinner?
3 What time does he/she eat?
4 What does he/she like doing? When? Where?
5 What would he/she like to do?
6 Does he/she do any exercise?

3 Find a student from the other two groups. Compare and swap your answers.

What do you think?

- Do all three people have a good diet? Do they eat a lot?
- What do *you* eat in a day? When?
- Would you like the food they eat in Australia/South Korea/Hungary?
- What suggestions can you make for a good diet?
  Eat lots of fruit and vegetables.
  Don't drink too much coffee.

Food we like

SCOTT MORGAN, AUSTRALIA

Name: Scott Morgan
Age: 35
Lives: Bondi Beach, Australia
Works: At the University of Sydney

Australians usually eat a big breakfast. We like sausages, bacon and eggs and lots of Vegemite on toast!

At 12.00 I have lunch. I usually just have a sandwich because I'm so busy. I'd like to eat in the university canteen more often – it has lots of different types of food from Thai curries to Mexican burritos.

In the evening and at the weekend we have BBQs. The weather is good in Australia and in the summer we cook a lot of our food outside. I like doing the cooking when we have a BBQ. My children love hamburgers and kebabs, and I do too! My wife doesn't like red meat but she loves chicken and fish. I always drink a nice cold beer with my burger. Then we go for a walk on the beach. Perfect!

Three people from different parts of the world describe what they eat every day.

MIN-JUN GANG, SOUTH KOREA

Name: Min-Jun Gang
Age: 26
Lives: Seoul, South Korea
Works: At Samsung Electronics

I get up early, at 6 o'clock, so I usually just drink a cup of *tisane*. We drink a lot of herbal tea in South Korea and tisanes are my favourite, they are very healthy.

I take the subway to work and eat an apple on the train. I always have an early lunch, usually around 11.30. I like *kimbap* – this is egg, ham or fish and vegetables in rice and seaweed. It's very good. Samsung has an excellent gym and I like going there after work. I'd like to go more often but I'm always very tired and hungry at the end of a long day.

In the evening I visit my mother. She likes cooking for me. She makes *jjigae* and *kimchi* – this is stew and cabbage with rice.

HANNA VARGA, HUNGARY

Name: Hanna Varga
Age: 42
Lives: Budapest, Hungary
Works: In a hotel

For Hungarian people, breakfast is a big meal. We think it is important to eat a good meal at the start of the day. My family has bread, sausage, cheese and peppers or tomatoes. Sometimes we eat bread and butter with jam, and we drink tea or cocoa.

I like riding my bike to work. Budapest is a beautiful city and it's a lovely start to my day. I'm a receptionist at a busy hotel in the city centre. I don't have time for lunch. I have a snack at about 2.00, usually a cheese and salami sandwich and a strong cup of coffee. I sometimes have some *rétes* too – a delicious strudel with fruit.

In the evening we have dinner at 8.00 – goulash or chicken paprikash and potatoes are our favourites.

I'd like to go for a run in the evening but I'm too tired and too busy. Maybe one day when I have more time!

Vocabulary and speaking
In a café

1 Complete the menu with the food and drink from the box below.

> Soup of the day ~~Soup of the day~~ Chocolate cake
> Cheese and ham   Fish and chips
> Green salad   Fresh fruit juice

2 🔊 12.9 Listen to Paul and Iris ordering a meal in Joe's Café. Who says these things? Write **P** (Paul), **I** (Iris), or **W** (Waiter).

_W__ Are you ready to order?

____ Well, I am. Are you ready, Iris?

____ Hmm – yes, I think so. What's the soup of the day?

____ Vegetable soup.

____ Lovely. I'd like the vegetable soup to start, please.

____ And to follow?

____ I'd like the salmon salad with some garlic bread on the side.

____ Thank you. And you, sir? What would you like?

____ Er – I'd like the toast and pâté, followed by hamburger and chips.

____ Would you like any side orders?

____ No, thank you. Just the hamburger.

____ And to drink?

____ Sparkling water for me, please. What about you, Paul?

____ The same for me. We'd like a large bottle of sparkling water, please.

____ Of course. I'll bring your drinks immediately.

3 🔊 12.9 Listen again. Practise the conversations in groups of three.

Role-play

4 Work in groups of three. Role-play being customers and waiters in a café.

Joe's Café

Starters
¹ _Soup of the day_	£4.50
Pâté with toast	£ 6.40

Mains
Salmon salad	£10.50
Hamburger and chips	£10.25
² _____	£10.75
Pizza – margherita/pepperoni	£9.95
Spaghetti Bolognese	£9.25

Sandwiches
³ _____	£5.25
Chicken and salad	£5.50
Egg and tomato	£5.95

Side orders
Chips	£3.00
⁴ _____	£3.00
Garlic bread	£3.00

Desserts
⁵ _____	£4.75
Apple pie and ice cream	£5.75

Drinks
Coke	£3.00
⁶ _____	£4.00
Tea	£2.50
Coffee	£3.00
Still or sparkling water	£2.50 (SMALL)
	£4.00 (LARGE)

OPEN 11 A.M. TILL 11 P.M.

📲 Go online for more **vocabulary** practice

Everyday English

Signs all around

1 Look at the signs. Where can you see them?

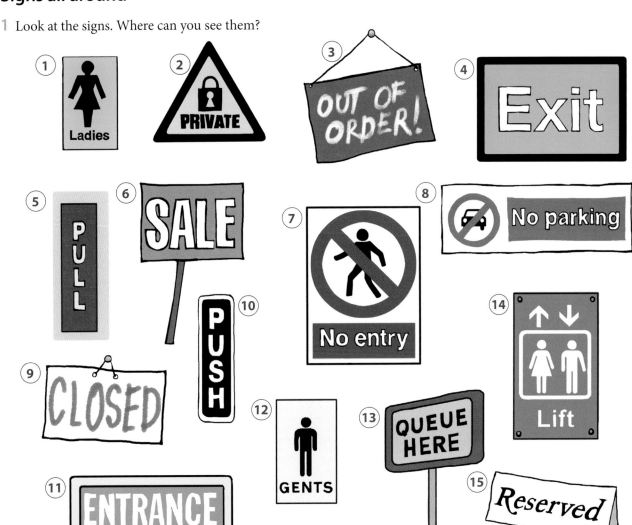

2 Which sign means … ?

1 ____ You can go in here.
2 ____ You can go out here.
3 ____ You can't sit here.
4 ____ You can't park here.
5 ____ This machine doesn't work.
6 ____ Push this door to open it.
7 ____ Pull this door to open it.

8 ____ Men can go to the toilet here.
9 ____ You can go up or down the floors here.
10 ____ Women can go to the toilet here.
11 ____ You can buy something cheap here.
12 ____ Stand and wait here.
13 ____ Not open.
14 ____ / ____ You can't go in here.

3 🔊 12.10 Listen to the lines of conversation. Which sign do they go with?

1 ____   2 ____   3 ____   4 ____   5 ____   6 ____   7 ____   8 ____

4 Work with a partner. Write a conversation that goes with a sign.   [→ Go online for more **speaking** practice
Act it out to the class. Can they identify the correct sign?

Grammar reference

➔ 12.1 would like

1   We use *would like* to ask for things.

Positive

I You He/She We They	**'d like**	a cup of tea.

2   We use *Would … like?* to offer things.

Question

Would	you he/she they	**like**	some cake?

3   Look at the answers.

Would you like a cup of tea?	*Yes, please.* *No, thank you.*

We use *would like*, not *want*, to be polite.

I'd like a coffee, please.   NOT   ~~I want a coffee.~~

4   We can use *would like* with another verb.

Would you **like to go out** tonight?
What **would** you **like to do**?

➔ 12.2 some and any

1   We use *some* in positive sentences.

I'd like		ham.
There's	**some**	cheese.
We have		books.

2   We use *any* in questions.

Is there		ham?
Do you have	**any**	money?
Are there		people?

3   We use *any* in negatives.

There isn't		bread.
We don't have	**any**	friends.
There aren't		books.

4   We use *some* when we offer things or ask for things.

Would you like Can I have	**some**	wine? cheese?

➔ 12.3 like and would like

1   We use *like* and *like doing* to talk about things we always like.

I **like** coffee.   (= I always enjoy coffee.)
She **likes** swimming in summer.   (=She always enjoys swimming.)

2   We use *would like* to talk about things we want now or soon.

I**'d like** a coffee.   (= I want a coffee.)
I**'d like** to go shopping.   (= I want to go shopping.)

Wordlist

adj = adjective	*n* = noun
adv = adverb	*phr* = phrase
conj = conjunction	*pl* = plural
prep = preposition	
pron = pronoun	
v = verb	

Anything else?   /ˌeniθɪŋ ˈels/   _____
apple pie   *n*   /ˌæpl ˈpaɪ/   _____
bacon   *n*   /ˈbeɪkən/   _____
bookshop   *n*   /ˈbʊkʃɒp/   _____
bottle   *n*   /ˈbɒtl/   _____
bread   *n*   /bred/   _____
butter   *n*   /ˈbʌtə(r)/   _____
cabbage   *n*   /ˈkæbɪdʒ/   _____
canteen   *n*   /kænˈtiːn/   _____
cocoa   *n*   /ˈkəʊkəʊ/   _____
curry   *n*   /ˈkʌri/   _____
customer   *n*   /ˈkʌstəmə(r)/   _____
dessert   *n*   /dɪˈzɜːt/   _____
diet   *n*   /ˈdaɪət/   _____
entrance   *n*   /ˈentrəns/   _____
entry   *n*   /ˈentri/   _____
exit   *n*   /ˈeksɪt/   _____
forget   *v*   /fəˈget/   _____
garlic bread   *n*   /ˈgɑːlɪk bred /   _____
gents   *n pl*   /dʒents/   _____
ham   *n*   /hæm/   _____
herbal tea   *n*   /ˈhɜːbl tiː/   _____
jam   *n*   /dʒæm/   _____
just   *adv*   /dʒʌst/   _____
kilo   *n*   /ˈkiːləʊ/   _____
ladies   *n pl*   /ˈleɪdiz/   _____
maybe   *adv*   /ˈmeɪbi/   _____
meat   *n*   /miːt/   _____
menu   *n*   /ˈmenjuː/   _____
order   *v*   /ˈɔːdə(r)/   _____
out of order   *phr*   /ˌaʊt əv ˈɔːdə(r)/   _____
pâté   *n*   /ˈpæteɪ/   _____
pepper   *n*   /ˈpepə(r)/   _____
potato   *n*   /pəˈteɪtəʊ/   _____
present   *n*   /ˈpreznt/   _____
private   *adj*   /ˈpraɪvət/   _____
pull   *v*   /pʊl/   _____
push   *v*   /pʊʃ/   _____
queue   *v*   /kjuː/   _____
reserved   *adj*   /rɪˈzɜːvd/   _____
rice   *n*   /raɪs/   _____
salami   *n*   /səˈlɑːmi/   _____
sale   *n*   /seɪl/   _____
salmon   *n*   /ˈsæmən/   _____
seaweed   *n*   /ˈsiːwiːd/   _____
side order   *n*   /ˈsaɪd ˌɔːdə(r)/   _____
sign   *n*   /saɪn/   _____
slice   *n*   /ˈslaɪs/   _____
snack   *n*   /snæk/   _____
soup   *n*   /suːp/   _____
sparkling water   *n*   /ˈspɑːklɪŋ wɔːtə(r)/   _____
starter   *n*   /ˈstɑːtə(r)/   _____
stew   *n*   /stjuː/   _____
still water   *n*   /ˈstɪl ˌwɔːtə(r)/   _____
subway   *n*   /ˈsʌbweɪ/   _____
too much   *phr*   /ˌtuː ˈmʌtʃ/   _____
wait   *v*   /weɪt/   _____

What's happening now?

13

- **Grammar** Present Continuous; Present Simple and Present Continuous
- **Vocabulary** Colours and clothes; Opposite verbs
- **Everyday English** What's the matter?
- **Reading** Today's different

Look at the photo. Answer the questions.

1 What can you see?

2 How many colours can you name?

What colour is it?

1 Write the colours.

| blue | ~~red~~ | green | black | white | yellow | brown | grey | orange | pink |

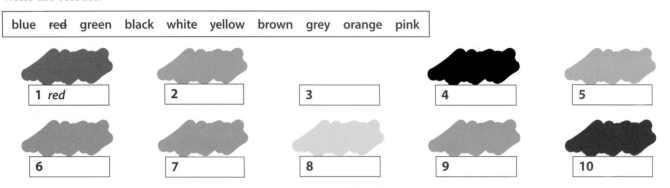

| 1 *red* | 2 | 3 | 4 | 5 |

| 6 | 7 | 8 | 9 | 10 |

2 What is your favourite colour? Tell the class.

Vocabulary
Clothes

1 What are the clothes? Write words from the box.

| a jacket   trousers   shoes and socks   a scarf   ~~a jumper~~   boots   trainers |
| a suit   a shirt and tie   a skirt   a dress   a T-shirt and shorts |

| 1 *a jumper* | 2 | 3 | 4 |

| 5 | 6 | 7 | 8 |

| 9 | 10 | 11 | 12 |

🔊 13.1 Listen and repeat.

2 Work with a partner. Describe the clothes.

> It's a blue jumper.

> They're white trainers.

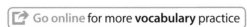
Go online for more **vocabulary** practice

Grammar
Present Continuous

1 Look at the picture and complete the descriptions with the clothes. Write the names of the people in the boxes.

1 **Polly** and **Penny** are wearing yellow *dresses* and pink _____ . They're eating ice cream.
2 **Carl**'s wearing a grey _____ and a white _____ . He's reading his emails.
3 **Lily**'s wearing an orange _____ and white _____ . She's running.
4 **Eva**'s wearing a green _____ and brown _____ . She's carrying a black bag.
5 **Rick**'s wearing blue _____ and a red _____ . He's playing the guitar.

🔊 13.2 Listen and check.

● **GRAMMAR SPOT**

1 **The Present Continuous** describes what is happening *now*.
   He**'s wearing** a grey suit.
   They**'re eating** ice cream.
   I**'m sitting** in the classroom.

🔊 13.3 Listen and repeat.

2 We make the **Present Continuous** with the verb
   to be: am/is/are + verb + *-ing*.
   Complete the sentences.
   I '*m studying* (*study*) English.
   You/We/They _____ (*wear*) jeans.
   She/He _____ (*play*) in the garden.

➔ Grammar reference 13.1 ▶ p130

2 🔊 13.4 Listen and repeat the questions.

What**'s** he **wearing**?
What **are** they **doing**? ?

Ask and answer the questions about the picture with a partner.

What's Carl wearing? A grey suit and …

What's he doing? He's …

3 Work with a partner. Describe someone in the room. Who is it?

He's wearing a white shirt, blue jeans. He's sitting next to me. It's Sergio.

4 Stand up and describe your clothes.

I'm wearing blue jeans and a black T-shirt.

Practice

Asking questions

1 Work with a partner. What are the people doing? Ask and answer questions.

> **What's he doing?** **He's cooking.**

🔊 **13.5** Listen and check. What extra information do you hear?

2 Mime actions to your partner. Can your partner guess what you are doing?

> **You're cooking!** **Yes, I am. I'm making a cake.**

> **You're playing tennis!** **No, I'm not. I'm playing golf.**

Grammar

Present Simple and Present Continuous

1 Read about Carl. Complete the text with the verbs in the box.

| go | has | ~~works~~ | reads | wears | arrives | feels |

CARL AT WORK

Carl is a businessman. He ¹*works* from 9.00 to 5.30 every day. He always ²_____ a suit and tie for work. He usually ³_____ lunch at his desk at 1.00. He ⁴_____ home at about 7.00 every evening and he ⁵_____ to his children before they ⁶_____ to bed. He often ⁷_____ very tired at the end of the day.

🔊 **13.6** Listen and check.

2 🔊 **13.7** Carl and his family are on holiday in Spain. Carl is talking to his boss, Brian, on his mobile phone. Listen to and read the conversation.

CARL ON HOLIDAY

Carl Hello.

Brian Carl, it's Brian, sorry to call you about work.

C Oh, hi, Brian! That's OK.

B First things first, **are** you **having** a good time?

C Yes, we are. We**'re having** a great time.

B **Are** you **staying** in a hotel?

C No, we're not. We**'re staying** in a villa with a swimming pool near the beach.

B Wonderful. And your family? **Are** they **enjoying** it?

C Oh, yes. The kids **are swimming** in the pool right now. Can you hear them?

B I can. And **are** you and your wife **relaxing**?

C We are. We**'re sitting** by the pool. Diane's **sunbathing** and I**'m reading** a lot – books and magazines, not reports! And it's great that I**'m not wearing** a suit and tie, just a T-shirt and shorts!

B You're lucky. It**'s raining** again here. Now, I**'m calling** about work …

C OK, Brian, what's the problem?

B Well …

3 How many true sentences can you make about Carl's holiday? Compare with your partner.

Carl		enjoying the holiday.
		talking to Brian.
Diane	is	calling Carl.
Brian	isn't	staying in a hotel.
The children	are	wearing a suit.
It	aren't	raining in Spain.
They		swimming in the pool.
		relaxing.

4 Work with a partner. Ask and answer the questions about Carl's holiday.

1 Are they … a good time?
2 Where … staying?
3 What … the children doing?
4 What … Diane doing?
5 What … Carl doing?
6 Is he … a suit?
7 Why … Brian calling?

> Are they having a good time?

> Yes, they are.

🔊 **13.8** Listen and check.

● **GRAMMAR SPOT**

Read the sentences.
   He **wears** a suit for work.
   He**'s wearing** a T-shirt.
Which sentence is about *now*?
Which is true every day but *not* now?

➔ Grammar reference 13.2 ▸ p130

5 Complete the sentences with the verbs in the Present Simple or Present Continuous.

1 Carl _lives_ (live) in a house in London, but now he _'s staying_ (stay) in a villa by the sea.
2 He usually _____ (wear) a suit, but today he _____ (wear) shorts.
3 He never _____ (relax) at work, but now he _____ (relax) by the pool.
4 Diane _____ (work) in a shop, but today she _____ (enjoy) her holiday.
5 The children _____ (work) hard at school, but today they _____ (swim) in the pool.
6 It often _____ (rain) in England and it _____ (rain) there now.

▶ Go online to **watch** a video about a charity clothes shop.

Practice

Questions and answers

1 Make the questions.

1 you / wear / a new jumper?
   Are you wearing a new jumper?
2 we / learn / Chinese?
3 we / sit / in a classroom?
4 you / listen / to the teacher?
5 the teacher / wear / blue trousers?
6 all the students / speak / English?
7 you / learn / a lot of English?
8 it / rain today?

Stand up. Ask and answer the questions.

> Are you wearing a new jumper?

> No, I'm not. It's really old.

A photo of you

2 Bring a photograph of you to class.
Say …

- where you are.
- what you're doing.
- who you're with.
- what you're wearing.

Check it

3 Tick (✓) the correct sentence.

1 ☐ I'm wear a blue shirt today.
  ☐ I'm wearing a blue shirt today.

2 ☐ Where are you going?
  ☐ Where you going?

3 ☐ Peter no working this week.
  ☐ Peter isn't working this week.

4 ☐ That's Peter over there. He talks to the teacher.
  ☐ That's Peter over there. He's talking to the teacher.

5 ☐ Heidi is German. She comes from Berlin.
  ☐ Heidi is German. She's coming from Berlin.

6 ☐ Why aren't you having a coffee?
  ☐ Why you no having a coffee?

⟳ Go online for more **grammar** practice

Reading and speaking
What are they doing?

1 What do you usually do on Saturday? On your birthday? On Christmas Day? On Sunday evening?

2 Look at the photos. Where are the people? What are they doing?

3 Work in two groups, **A** and **B**.

| Group A | Read about **Mark** and **Isabel**. |
| Group B | Read about **Jia** and **Leo**. |

Answer the questions about your people.

1 What day is it?
2 What does he/she usually do on this day?
3 Why is today different?
4 What is he/she doing?
5 What happened this morning?
6 What is he/she wearing?

4 Find a partner from the other group. Use the questions and the photos to tell each other about your two people.

What do you think?

Read these lines. Which of the four people do you think wrote them? Who to?

1

> I'm sitting on the plane at last. I'm doing some work preparing for my meetings. I forgot to bring the annual report. Can you email it to me?

2

> Hi guys! Thanks for coming! It's two o'clock in the morning now and I'm going to bed at last. I had a great time! I hope you all did.

3

> Thank you for everything, Mum and Dad! It was a great day! We're driving to the airport now. I'm so excited – Barbados tomorrow. Love you!

4

> Thanks for the fabulous hamburgers. I'm still full! Do you know it's snowing back home? I can't believe it!

Today's different!

Mark

"On Christmas Day we usually all go to my parents' house. We open our presents, then have a big lunch at about 2.00 in the afternoon."

But this Christmas is different!

Mark and his wife are in Australia. They're visiting friends. This morning they went to the beach, and now they're having a Christmas barbecue next to the swimming pool. It's hot and they're wearing T-shirts and shorts.

Isabel

"On Saturday mornings I usually get up late and do the housework. Then I meet some friends in town for lunch, and go shopping in the afternoon."

But this Saturday is different!

This morning Isabel got up early because today is her wedding day. She's with all her family and friends in church and she's getting married. She's wearing a white dress, and her new husband is standing next to her. A lot of people are taking photos.

Jia

"I work in a busy office in the centre of Beijing. I usually hate Sunday evenings because that's when I get ready for my week at work."

But this Sunday evening is different!

Jia's getting ready to go on a business trip to London tomorrow.

This morning she practised her English then she had lunch with friends. Now she is packing her bags. She's trying on a new suit. She's enjoying this Sunday evening because she's so excited about her trip.

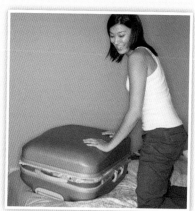

Leo

"On my birthday I sometimes go out with friends, or I go out to a restaurant with my family. My Mum usually makes me a birthday cake."

But this birthday is different!

It's Leo's eighteenth birthday, so now he's an adult. This morning he got a lot of presents. Now he's having a big party with all his friends. They're dancing and drinking beer. Leo's wearing a white T-shirt.

Vocabulary and listening
Opposite verbs

1 Look at the two sentences. <u>Underline</u> the verbs. They are verbs with opposite meaning.

The teacher's asking us questions.   **We're answering them.**

2 Match the verbs with their opposites.

play   sell   hate   turn off   ~~arrive~~   finish   forget   take off   go to bed   lose   run   close

1 leave *arrive*
2 work _____
3 buy _____

4 walk _____
5 love _____
6 open _____

7 turn on _____
8 start _____
9 get up _____

10 remember _____
11 put on _____
12 win _____

3 Look at the pictures. Complete the sentences with the opposite verb in the correct form.

1 Please, don't **ask** me any more questions. I can't _____ them.

2 I'm **selling** my old car and I'm _____ a new one.

3 We always **get up** at 7:00 in the morning and _____ at 11:00 at night.

4 It was cold, so Tom **took off** his T-shirt and _____ a warm jumper.

5 I usually **walk** to school, but yesterday I was late so I _____ all the way.

6 John's playing tennis with Peter today. He always **loses**. He never _____ .

7 Don't **turn off** the TV, I'm watching it! Please _____ it _____ again!

13.9 Listen and check.

4 **13.10** Listen. Write down the opposite verbs in each conversation.

1 *hate* , *love*   2 _____ , _____   3 _____ , _____   4 _____ , _____   5 _____ , _____   6 _____ , _____

Look at audioscript 13.10 on page 144. Practise the conversations.

Look at audioscript 13.10 on page 144.

↗ Go online for more **vocabulary** practice

Everyday English
What's the matter?

1 What's the matter with the people? Complete the sentences with words in the box.

bored   hungry   thirsty   ~~cold~~   hot   tired   worried   angry   a cold   a headache

1 She's *cold*.

2 He's _____.

3 They're _____.

4 He's _____.

5 They're _____.

6 She's _____.

7 He's _____.

8 She's _____.

9 He has _____.

10 She has _____.

🔊 13.11 Listen and repeat.

2 Complete the conversations with words from exercise 1.

1

A What's the matter?
B I'm ¹_____ and ²_____.
A Why don't you have a cup of tea?
B That's a good idea.
A Sit down. I'll make it for you.

2

C What's the matter?
D I have a bad ³_____.
C Oh dear! Why don't you take some aspirin?
D I don't have any.
C It's OK. I have some.

🔊 13.12 Listen and check. Practise the conversations with a partner.

Role-play

3 Have similar conversations. Use the words from exercise 1 and these ideas.

- go to bed early
- put on a jumper
- have a sandwich
- have a cold drink
- talk to a friend
- watch a film
- sit down and relax
- go to the cinema
- have a cold shower

↗ **Go online** for more **speaking** practice

Grammar reference

13.1 Present Continuous

Positive

I	am	
He She It	is	**working.**
You We They	are	

Negative

I	'm not	
He She It	isn't	**working.**
You We They	aren't	

Questions with question words

	am I	
What	**are** you **are** we **are** they	**wearing?**
	is he **is** she	

Yes/No questions and short answers

Are you **wearing** jeans?	Yes, I **am**. No, I **'m not**.
Is she **reading** a newspaper?	Yes, she **is**. No, she **isn't**.

13.2 Present Simple and Present Continuous

1 We use the Present Simple to talk about actions that are true for all time or a long time.

> Hans **comes** from Germany.
> I **love** you.
> My father **works** in a bank.
> I **get up** at 7.30 every day.
> She **doesn't understand** French.

2 We use the Present Continuous to talk about actions that last a short time. The actions are happening now.

> I usually wear jeans, but today I**'m wearing** a suit.
> He speaks French very well. He**'s speaking** French to that man.
> It**'s raining**.
> They**'re swimming**.
> We**'re playing** football.

Wordlist

adj = adjective	n = noun	pl = plural
adv = adverb	phr = phrase	pron = pronoun
conj = conjunction	phr v = phrasal verb	v = verb

adult   n /ˈædʌlt/   _____
angry   adj /ˈæŋgri/   _____
at the moment   phr /ət ðə ˈməʊmənt/ _____
boots   n pl /buːts/   _____
bored   adj /bɔːd/   _____
bring   v /brɪŋ/   _____
carry   v /ˈkærɪ/   _____
close   v /kləʊz/   _____
cold   adj /kəʊld/   _____
colour   n /ˈkʌlə(r)/   _____
dress   n /dres/   _____
end   n /end/   _____
extra   adj /ˈekstrə/   _____
finish   v /ˈfɪnɪʃ/   _____
guess   v /ges/   _____
happen   v /ˈhæpən/   _____
have a cold   phr /hæv ə ˈkəʊld/   _____
headache   n /ˈhedeɪk/   _____
housework   n /ˈhaʊswɜːk/   _____
hungry   adj /ˈhʌŋgri/   _____
lose   v /luːz/   _____
open   v /ˈəʊpən/   _____
pack   v /pæk/   _____
plane   n /pleɪn/   _____
practise   v /ˈpræktɪs/   _____
put on   phr v /pʊt ˈɒn/   _____
remember   v /rɪˈmembə(r)/   _____
scarf   n /skɑːf/   _____
sell   v /sel/   _____
shirt   n /ʃɜːt/   _____
shorts   n pl /ʃɔːts/   _____
skirt   n /skɜːt/   _____
socks   n pl /sɒks/   _____
someone   pron /ˈsʌmwʌn/   _____
suit   n /suːt/   _____
take off   phr v /teɪk ˈɒf/   _____
thirsty   adj /ˈθɜːsti/   _____
tie   n /taɪ/   _____
trip   n /trɪp/   _____
trousers   n pl /ˈtraʊzəz/   _____
turn on   phr v /tɜːn ˈɒn/   _____
turn off   phr v /tɜːn ˈɒf/   _____
wear   v /ˈweə(r)/   _____
win   v /wɪn/   _____
worried   v /ˈwʌrid/   _____

Colours
black   adj /blæk/   _____
blue   adj /bluː/   _____
brown   adj /braʊn/   _____
green   adj /griːn/   _____
grey   adj /greɪ/   _____
orange   adj /ˈɒrɪndʒ/   _____
pink   adj /pɪŋk/   _____
red   adj /red/   _____
white   adj /waɪt/   _____
yellow   adj /ˈjeləʊ/   _____

Let's go! 14

Look at the photo. Answer the questions.

1 Where are the people?

2 What are they doing? Where are they going?

3 What are the people wearing?

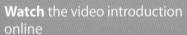

Ready, steady, go!

1 Write the forms of transport.

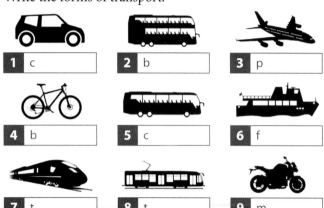

1 c		**2** b		**3** p	
4 b		**5** c		**6** f	
7 t		**8** t		**9** m	

2 How do you travel? Where to?

I usually come to school by bus, but today I came by car. Sometimes I travel by …

Grammar

Future plans

1 Stewart and Geoff are from New Zealand but they are in the UK now. They want to travel round Europe and North Africa. They have just one week! Look at the map and answer the questions.

1 Which countries are they visiting?
2 Where does the holiday begin? Where does it end?
3 How are they travelling?

2 Read the holiday information and check your answers.

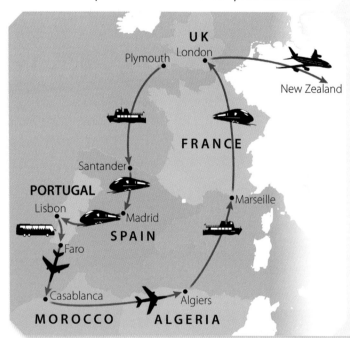

Seven countries in seven days

1 **SATURDAY** **PLYMOUTH, ENGLAND – SANTANDER, SPAIN**

Overnight ferry to Santander.

2 **SUNDAY** **SANTANDER – MADRID**

Train to Madrid. Check in to hotel. Bus tour of Madrid, visit to Royal Palace, Prado National Museum. Have sangria and tapas in the evening.

3 **MONDAY** **MADRID – LISBON, PORTUGAL**

Early morning start. Train through Spain and into Portugal to Lisbon. Afternoon sightseeing. Evening boat cruise on River Tagus. Overnight in Lisbon.

4 **TUESDAY** **LISBON – FARO**

By coach to Faro. Afternoon on the beach. Go to a nightclub.

5 **WEDNESDAY** **FARO – CASABLANCA, MOROCCO**

Early morning start. Fly to Casablanca. Drive through the old town and stop at Hassan 11 Mosque. Have dinner in the Quartier Habous. Overnight in Casablanca.

The 25 de Abril Bridge, Lisbon

Hassan II Mosque, Casablanca

6 THURSDAY CASABLANCA – ALGIERS, ALGERIA

Have breakfast at one of Casablanca's famous cafés then fly to Algiers. Visit the Notre Dame D'Afrique and have a late lunch after walking through the Garden of Essai du Hamma. Overnight in Algiers.

7 FRIDAY ALGIERS – MARSEILLE, FRANCE

Late morning ferry across the Mediterranean Sea to Marseille, France. Arrive on Saturday morning.

8 SATURDAY MARSEILLE – LONDON – AUCKLAND, NEW ZEALAND

Arrive in Marseille. Walk round the spice market and the old port. Visit the Basilique Notre Dame de la Garde. Have seafood dinner in the evening by the sea. Overnight Eurostar from Marseille to London. Arrive at St Pancras Station, London at 6.30 on Sunday morning. Flight back to New Zealand from London Heathrow.

● **GRAMMAR SPOT**

Here are two ways of talking about future plans.

1 Present Continuous
They**'re leaving** on Saturday at six o'clock.
We**'re flying** to New York tomorrow/next week.

2 *going to*
They**'re going to have** a boat cruise on the River Tagus.
We**'re going to walk** round the old port.

→ **Grammar reference 14.1** > **p140**

3 Read the holiday information again carefully. Complete the sentences.

1 On Saturday they're getting the overnight _____ to Santander.
2 On Sunday they're going to have a _____ tour of Madrid.
3 On Monday they're travelling by _____ through Spain and into Portugal.
4 On Tuesday they're _____ to get the coach to Faro.
5 On Wednesday they're going to _____ to Casablanca.
6 On Thursday they're going to _____ breakfast in Casablanca then they're _____ to Algiers.
7 On Friday they're getting the _____ morning ferry to Marseille.
8 On Saturday they're _____ to have dinner by the sea and then they're getting the _____ Eurostar to London.

🔊 **14.1** Listen and check.

Questions

4 🔊 **14.2** Listen and repeat the questions.

> What **are** they **doing** on Sunday?
> What **are** they **going to do** on Monday?

❓

5 Complete the questions about Stewart and Geoff.

1 When / going to have / sangria and tapas?
2 What / going to do / Lisbon?
3 What / doing / Tuesday?
4 What / going to do / Wednesday?
5 Where / having dinner / Wednesday?
6 When / going to Marseille?
7 When / arriving back / London?

🔊 **14.3** Listen and check. Ask and answer the questions with a partner.

6 🔊 **14.4** Listen to four conversations. Where are Stewart and Geoff?

1 _____   3 _____
2 _____   4 _____

▶ **Go online** to **watch** a video where people talk about their holiday plans.

Practice

Evie's plans

1 **Evie** is talking to her friend **Freya** about her holiday plans. Complete the conversation with the question words.

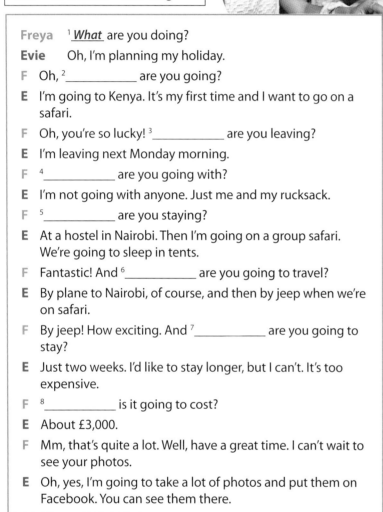

| when | where (x2) | ~~what~~ | who |
| how | how much | how long | |

Freya   ¹ *What* are you doing?

Evie   Oh, I'm planning my holiday.

F   Oh, ² _____ are you going?

E   I'm going to Kenya. It's my first time and I want to go on a safari.

F   Oh, you're so lucky! ³ _____ are you leaving?

E   I'm leaving next Monday morning.

F   ⁴ _____ are you going with?

E   I'm not going with anyone. Just me and my rucksack.

F   ⁵ _____ are you staying?

E   At a hostel in Nairobi. Then I'm going on a group safari. We're going to sleep in tents.

F   Fantastic! And ⁶ _____ are you going to travel?

E   By plane to Nairobi, of course, and then by jeep when we're on safari.

F   By jeep! How exciting. And ⁷ _____ are you going to stay?

E   Just two weeks. I'd like to stay longer, but I can't. It's too expensive.

F   ⁸ _____ is it going to cost?

E   About £3,000.

F   Mm, that's quite a lot. Well, have a great time. I can't wait to see your photos.

E   Oh, yes, I'm going to take a lot of photos and put them on Facebook. You can see them there.

🔊 **14.5** Listen and check. Practise the conversation with a partner.

2 Ask and answer questions about Evie's holiday plans with your partner.

- Where / going?
- Why / going?
- Who / going with?
- When / leaving?
- How / going to travel?
- Where / going to stay?
- How long / going to stay?

> Where's she going?

> She's going to Kenya.

> Why is she going there?

> Because …

Talking about you

3 Work in pairs. Ask and answer questions about your plans. Ask about …

- after the lesson
- this evening
- tomorrow
- this weekend
- your next holiday

> What are you doing/going to do after the lesson?

Check it

4 Each sentence has one word missing. Write it in.

1 What you doing this evening?   *(are)*
2 I'm going see some friends tonight.
3 When they going to France?
4 She seeing the doctor tomorrow.
5 What time are you to leave?
6 I going to the cinema on Saturday evening.

> ↪ **Go online** for more **grammar** practice

Vocabulary revision
Words that go together

1 Match a verb in **A** with words in **B**.

A	B
play	hard
travel	a photo
drive	by train
go	dinner with friends
work	cards
have	cycling
take	carefully
do	a suit
pay	your homework
wear	bills online

Work with a partner. Talk about your plans.

> I'm going cycling at the weekend.

2 Draw a line between words that have a connection.

Explain the connection.
Trains travel between stations.

station — journalist
shampoo
newspaper → train
airport
hospital
sunbathing
waiter
kitchen
fridge menu
nurse beach
chemist's
planes

3 Three words belong to a group and one is different.
<u>Underline</u> the one that is different. Why is it different?

1	train	bus	<u>bridge</u>	motorbike
2	wife	waiter	daughter	grandfather
3	lovely	fantastic	amazing	awful
4	trainers	trousers	socks	boots
5	desk	armchair	sofa	laptop
6	actor	journalist	cooker	builder

Pronunciation

4 🔊 14.6 Listen and write the words in the correct box.
Two syllables

~~pilot~~ ~~hotel~~ women married chocolate
enjoy shampoo arrive

●●	●●
pilot	hotel

🔊 14.7 Listen and check.

5 🔊 14.8 Listen and write the words in the correct box.
Three syllables

~~photograph~~ ~~amazing~~ assistant vegetable
~~magazine~~ interesting understand banana
souvenir

●●●	●●●	●●●
photograph	amazing	magazine

🔊 14.9 Listen and check.

6 🔊 14.10 Listen and <u>underline</u> the two words that rhyme.

1	<u>some</u>	home	<u>come</u>
2	goes	knows	does
3	were	here	her
4	make	steak	speak
5	near	wear	there
6	eat	great	wait

🔊 14.10 Listen again and check.

> ➦ Go online for more **vocabulary** practice

Reading and speaking
Life's big events

1 Put these life events into an order.

____ went to school
_1_ was born …
____ got married
____ grew up …
____ studied at university
____ met a boyfriend/girlfriend

2 🔊 14.11 Look at the pictures of Milena Dušek, Georg Reinhardt, and Archie McCrae.

Listen to them talk about their lives. Who talks about …?

• his/her parents
• his/her girlfriend/boyfriend/husband/wife
• his/her studies
• where he/she lives

What do they say?

3 Work in three groups.

Group A Read about **Milena Dušek**.

Group B Read about **Georg Reinhardt**.

Group C Read about **Archie McCrae**.

Read your text quickly. Find one piece of information about his/her past, present, and future. Compare your ideas in your group.

4 Read your text again and answer the questions.

1 Where was he/she born?
2 Where … live? Who … with?
3 Where … grow up?
4 What … parents/wife do?
5 Where … go to school?
6 What … study/studying at school/university?
7 When … going abroad?
8 What … going to do there?
9 How does … feel about going?

Find a student from the other two groups. Compare and swap information.

My past, present
Three people talk about their family,

Milena Dušek

Georg Reinhardt

Archie McCrae

and **future**

education, work and ambitions.

Milena Dušek is Czech. She was born in Prague, where she still lives with her mother and two sisters. She's 18, and she goes to an international school. She is studying English, psychology and economics.

> 'My parents are divorced. My father is a journalist, and works for a newspaper called *Blesk*. My mother works as a chef in a restaurant in the Old Town. I see my father quite often. He lives nearby.'

Milena wants to work in banking. She's going to study business when she's older, so it's important that she speaks very good English. Next summer she's going to London for two months to study at a language school. She's going to stay with an English family, and she's going to learn English for five hours a day. She's excited about going to London, but a little bit worried, too.
She says,

> 'I hope the family are nice, and I hope I like English food!'

Georg Reinhardt is an architect. He's married, and he lives with his wife, Karlotta, and three children, in Berlin. Karlotta is a housewife, and their three children go to a local gymnasium (school).

> 'I was born in Frankfurt, where I grew up and went to school. I studied architecture at the University of Munich. I met Karlotta at university, she was a student of modern languages. We moved to Berlin in 1995.'

Georg also teaches architecture. Next year he is moving to America, to teach at the University of California in Berkeley for three years. His family is going with him. They're going to live on the university campus, where there is a school for the children. His wife is going to teach German. They're all very excited.
Georg says,

> 'The kids are learning English. They want to see the Golden Gate Bridge in San Francisco. My wife and I are looking forward to living in the sun all year round.'

Archie McCrae is Scottish. He was born in Glasgow, where he grew up with his parents and his brother and sister. His father is a doctor and his mother works for the research company, Bayer.

> 'I went to Drumchapel High School. I studied biology, chemistry and physics. At school I met Fiona, and we started going out when we were 16. We studied medicine together at the University of Edinburgh, and now we live in Edinburgh.'

Archie and Fiona want to work in developing countries. Next week they're going to Zambia, in Southern Africa, for a year to work in St Francis' Hospital in the east of the country. They're going to train doctors and nurses in villages near the hospital. How do they feel about their trip? Archie says,

> 'We're very excited, but a bit nervous. Zambia is a beautiful country, but poor. The people are wonderful. I hope we can help them.'

Talking about you

5 When we meet someone for the first time, we sometimes say a little bit about ourselves.

> I was born in …   I go to school in …

Find the expressions in the box in the texts about Milena, Georg, and Archie. <u>Underline</u> them.

> was born   grew up   live with   going to
> hope   work as/for   studying/studied
> excited about

6 Use the expressions in exercise 5 to write sentences about you.

7 Work with a partner. Imagine you are meeting for the first time. Tell him/her about yourself.

Ask questions to learn more about him/her.

> Where did you … ?   When did you … ?
> What are you going to … ?

Grammar revision
Tenses

1 Complete the sentences about Archie McCrae from page 137 with the verbs in the correct tense.

1 Archie and Fiona _live_ (live) in Edinburgh.
2 Archie _____ (have) a brother and a sister.
3 His mother _____ (work) for a research company, Bayer.
4 Archie _____ (grow up) in Glasgow.
5 He _____ (study) medicine at university.
6 He and Fiona _____ (go) to work in Zambia soon.

Questions

2 Complete the questions about Archie.

1 Where _do Archie and Fiona live?_
   They live in Edinburgh.
2 How many _____?
   Two, one brother and one sister.
3 Who _____ for?
   A research company called 'Bayer'.
4 Where did _____?
   In Glasgow.
5 What _____?
   Medicine.
6 Where are _____?
   Zambia.

Check it

3 Correct the mistakes.

          comes
1 He ~~come~~ from Canada.
          do
2 Where | you live?
3 I no want to go out.
4 She has 18 years old.
5 I went in Italy last year.
6 He have a dog and a cat.
7 I no can understand you.
8 What did you last night?
9 I going see a film tonight.
10 What you do this weekend?

4 Choose the correct answer.

1 I have _some_ homework to do this evening.
   a any   **b** some
2 In our town _____ a big park.
   a there's   **b** it's
3 Who is _____ man talking to Jane?
   a this   **b** that
4 I don't have _____ money. Sorry.
   a any   **b** some
5 Ann, _____ is my brother, Pete.
   Pete, _____ is Ann.
   a this   **b** that
6 My brother Pete is _____ actor.
   a a   **b** an
7 My _____ name is Alice.
   a mothers   **b** mother's
8 You speak _____.
   a English very well **b** very well English
9 I have a _____.
   a car German   **b** German car
10 I'm hungry. _____ a sandwich.
   a I'd like   **b** I like

Everyday English
Social expressions (2)

1 🔊 **14.12** Listen and look at the pictures. Complete the conversations with the words in the boxes.

| best | later | luck |

A Good _____ in the exam!
I hope it goes well.
B Thanks. I'll do my _____ .
A See you _____ . Bye!

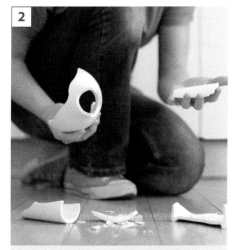

| matter | so | worry |

C Oh, no!
D Don't _____ . It doesn't _____ .
C I'm _____ sorry!

| weekend | Same | special |

E Have a good _____ !
F Thanks! _____ to you!
What are you doing? Anything _____ ?
E We're going to a birthday party.

| soon | text |

G Goodbye! Drive carefully!
H Thanks! I'll _____ you when I arrive.
G See you _____ !

| kind | present | to say |

I I have a _____ for you.
J For me? Why?
I It's just _____ thank you.
J That's so _____ of you!

| pleasure | everything | Bye |

K _____ ! And thanks for _____ !
L It was a _____ . We enjoyed having you.

🔊 **14.12** Listen again and check.

2 Work in pairs. Learn the conversations. Stand up! Act out the conversations to the class.

⤴ Go online for more **speaking** practice

Grammar reference

→ 14.1 Future plans

Positive

Present Continuous

I'm You're He's She's We're They're	**going** to Europe. **leaving** next week. **flying** on Sunday.

Going to

I'm You're He's She's We're They're	**going to**	**see** Buckingham Palace. **have** a tour of the city **stay** in the Ritz hotel.

Negative

Present Continuous

I'm **not** You **aren't** He **isn't** She **isn't** We **aren't** They **aren't**	**living** in London. **studying** medicine.

Going to

I'm **not** You **aren't** He **isn't** She **isn't** We **aren't** They **aren't**	**going to**	**travel** by train. **sleep** in a tent.

Questions

Present Continuous

Where When Where Who	**are** you	**going** on holiday? **leaving**? **staying**? **going** with?

Going to

Where What	**are** you **going to**	**stay**? **do**?

140   Unit 14 • Let's go!

Wordlist

adj = adjective	*n* = noun	*pl* = plural
adv = adverb	*phr* = phrase	*pron* = pronoun
conj = conjunction	*phr v* = phrasal verb	*v* = verb

abroad   *adv* /ə'brɔːd/   _____

across   *adv* /ə'krɒs/   _____

all year round   *phr* /ˌɔːl jɪə 'raʊnd/   _____

banana   *n* /bə'nɑːnə/   _____

begin   *v* /bɪ'gɪn/   _____

biology   *n* /baɪ'ɒlədʒi/   _____

boat   *n* /bəʊt/   _____

bridge   *n* /brɪdʒ/   _____

campus   *n* /'kæmpəs/   _____

carefully   *adv* /'keəfəli/   _____

check in   *phr v* /ˌtʃek 'ɪn/   _____

chemistry   *n* /'kemɪstri/   _____

cruise   *n* /kruːz/   _____

Czech   *adj* /tʃek/   _____

developing countries   *n pl* /dɪˌveləpɪŋ 'kʌntriz/   _____

divorced   *adj* /dɪ'vɔːst/   _____

economics   *n* /ˌiːkə'nɒmɪks/   _____

Europe   *n* /'jʊərəp/   _____

event   *n* /ɪ'vent/   _____

explain   *v* /ɪk'spleɪn/   _____

flight   *n* /flaɪt/   _____

future   *n* /'fjuːtʃə(r)/   _____

grow up   *phr v* /ˌgrəʊ 'ʌp/   _____

hope   *v* /həʊp/   _____

hostel   *n* /'hɒstl/   _____

housewife   *n* /'haʊswaɪf/   _____

how long?   /ˌhaʊ 'lɒŋ/   _____

imagine   *v* /ɪ'mædʒɪn/   _____

jeep   *n* /dʒiːp/   _____

journalist   *n* /'dʒɜːnəlɪst/   _____

local   *adj* /'ləʊkl/   _____

medicine   *n* /'medsn/   _____

motorbike   *n* /'məʊtəbaɪk/   _____

move   *v* /muːv/   _____

nearby   *adv* /nɪə'baɪ/   _____

overnight   *adv* /ˌəʊvə'naɪt/   _____

physics   *n* /'fɪzɪks/   _____

piece of information   *n* /ˌpiːs əv ɪnfə'meɪʃn/   _____

plan   *n,v* /plæn/   _____

pleasure   *n* /'pleʒə(r)/   _____

port   *n* /pɔːt/   _____

psychology   *n* /saɪ'kɒlədʒi/   _____

quickly   *adv* /'kwɪkli/   _____

research company   *n* /rɪ'sɜːtʃ ˌkʌmpəni/   _____

revision   *n* /rɪ'vɪʒn/   _____

rucksack   *n* /'rʌksæk/   _____

safari   *n* /sə'fɑːri/   _____

Same to you   /ˌseɪm tə 'juː/   _____

souvenir   *n* /ˌsuːvə'nɪə(r)/   _____

spice market   *n* /'spaɪs ˌmɑːkɪt/   _____

transport   *n* /'trænspɔːt/   _____

Pairwork

Unit 2 p18

Cities and countries

2 Work with a partner.

> **Student A** Look at the photos on p18.
>
> **Student B** Look at the photos on this page.

Ask and answer questions to complete the information.

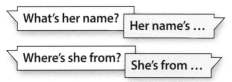

What's her name? / Her name's …

Where's she from? / She's from …

Student A	Student B
1  Her name's Steph. She's from New York.	**5**  *His name's …* *He's …*
2  His name's Érico. He's from Rio de Janeiro.	**6** 
3  Her name's Orlena. She's from Paris.	**7** 
4  His name's Ramses. He's from Cairo.	**8** 

Unit 8 p75

Two different kitchens

3 Work with a partner.

> **Student A** Look at the picture on p75.
> **Student B** Look at the picture on this page.
> Your pictures are different. Talk about your pictures to find seven differences.

Audioscripts

Unit 3

3.11 Scottish Rovers in Paris

I = interviewer, S = Shona, G = Gillian, All = Shona, Gillian, Emma, Fiona and Kate

I Good morning girls. How are you?
All Morning! All good thanks.
I So, is this your first time in Paris?
All Yes, it is. It's amazing here! We love it!
I Good! Now, you're all Scottish. Is that right?
All Yes. That's right. We're all from Scotland. Come on Scotland!
I Yes. Come on Scotland. Shona, you're the captain. How old are you?
S I'm 25. Emma, Fiona and Kate are 23 and Gillian is my sister …
I Is Gillian is 23, too?
G No, I'm not, I'm 25 like Shona.
I Uh! So you're sisters and you're both 25?
S&G Yes, we're twins! But we aren't identical twins!
I You're twins! Well, how interesting!
S&G Yes, but we are very different.
I Yes, you are. You aren't identical at all! Right. Now, who's married in the team?
All We're not married!
S But I am!
I Ah Shona, the captain. You're married. What's your husband's name?
S His name's Tom and he's a bus driver. He isn't here today, he's in Scotland.
I I see. Well, good luck in the final girls and enjoy Paris!
All Thank you.

Unit 5

5.6 Dexter and Daisy

I = Interviewer, Dex = Dexter, D = Daisy

I Dexter and Daisy. You're brother and sister. Do you like the same things?
D Well, I sometimes don't like Dexter when he's horrible to me …
I Well – he is your big brother!
D Yeah! … But we both really like ice cream. It's great.
Dex Yeah!
I What else do you like?
Dex Well, we both like chocolate.
D Mmm. I love chocolate. Chocolate is delicious – 'specially chocolate milkshake!
Dex Yeah! We both like milkshake. It's fantastic.
I So … What don't you like?
Dex Well, we definitely don't like tomatoes, do we, Daisy? Tomatoes are horrible!
D Yuk! I hate tomatoes. They're disgusting.
I Do you both like sports?
Dex Yes, we do. We like tennis – we play on Saturday mornings.
D Yes. We like tennis a lot. It's really exciting.
Dex And I love baseball, and Daddy loves it too. It's really cool!
I Do you like baseball Daisy?
D No, I don't! Baseball is boring!
Dex No, it isn't!!

5.9 Conversations with Alek

1 **Alek** Bye, Bella. Bye, Danek. Have a good day at school. I'm off to work now.
Danek Bye, Daddy. Have a good day, too.
Bella Alek! Your sandwiches!
Alek Oh yes! Thanks, honey. See you later.

2 **Alek** Good morning, sir. Do you want the £10 or £20 car wash?
Man What do I get for £10?
Alek We wash the outside, but we don't clean the inside.
Man OK, I see – and for £20 – inside and out?
Alek Yes, sir. We do a good job!
Man Fine. £20 it is.

3 **Dance teacher** Good evening, class. Today I want you to dance the Salsa. Your partners, please.
Bella Come on, Alek!
Dance teacher Are you all ready? Good. Now left turn.
Alek Ouch! Bella, my foot!!!
Bella Oops! Sorry, Alek.

4 **Alek** Brrr! It's cold today.
Danek I don't care! Come on, Bristol Rovers!
Alek Oh no! A goal for Chelsea.
Danek Come on, Bristol Rovers! Come on! They have the ball now, Dad!
Alek and Danek Hooray. Fantastic!! A great goal!

5.13 Party time

D = Daniel, T = Tam

D Hi there! Er, I think I know you? Oh – you're Tam, is that right?
T Hi! Yes I am, and you're … er … oh yes – Daniel! Hello again, Daniel.
D Hi! Good to see you again, Tam.
T You too.
D Now, I know you're not English, but you speak English very well. Where do you come from?
T Thank you. I'm from Korea, from Seoul. And you, Daniel, where are you from? London?
D No, I'm American. I live in Boston. I don't live in London, but I often come to London on business.
T I'm here on business, too. I come to London two or three times a year, but I also work in America, usually in New York.
D Really? I know New York well. Do you like it there?
T I do, I love working there – it's an exciting city. My company has offices all over the world so I often work in Berlin and Paris, too.
D What an interesting job! I don't know Berlin or Paris. So, do you speak French and German?
T I speak French but I don't speak it very well.
D I don't know any foreign languages!
T Oh dear!
D This is a great party … and I don't usually like parties. Great music! Do you like dancing, Tam?
T I love parties and I love dancing!
D Yeah, I like it too, but I don't dance very well.
T That doesn't matter! Come on! I want to dance!

Unit 8

8.7 A phone call with Jack's mum

J = Jack, M = Mum

M Hi, Jack! It's Mum. How are you? How's your new flat?
J Hi, Mum. It's great. I love it. It's really big and comfortable.
M And tidy?
J Er, well … My living room is tidy, but my bedroom …
M Hmm. Yes. So tell me more. Is there a nice sofa?
J There are two sofas! Black ones! They're really cool.
M OK. Black sofas – lovely. Are there any chairs?
J Yes. There's an old armchair, you know, my favourite one.
M Not that old thing! And a TV? Is there a TV?
J Yes, of course. A big one on the wall and a PlayStation and …
M A big TV? And a PlayStation? Oh dear!
J Mum, I love playing my football games.
M Mmm. I know you do. And is there a desk in the bedroom?
J No, there isn't one in the bedroom. There's one in the living room.
N Oh good!
J My living room is big and there's a great view of the park from my window.
M Oh, nice. And do you have any pictures on the wall?
J Hmm. No, but there are my favourite David Bowie posters. Oh, and some nice photos of you and Dad.
M Really! OK. Now, your dad and I want to see this flat. Is next Saturday OK?
J Visit? Next Saturday? … er … I'm very busy, Mum, … er …
M Good. See you next Saturday then. Bye, love.
J Bye, Mum.

8.11 My home town

Hi! My name's Ben, and I live in Cape Town. I'm a DJ at a local radio station in the centre of the city, but I live near Boulders Beach – one of the best beaches in Cape Town. I have a small apartment near there. Cape Town is an amazing city. It's really cosmopolitan. People from all over the world live and work here. Every Friday after work I meet my friends at the Waterfront, and we go to one of the restaurants there. We often have seafood – it's my favourite. I just love fresh seafood.
The weather's great, it's warm nearly all year round. I know it's sometimes windy – and some people don't like the wind – but I love it because I love kitesurfing! My job's really exciting, but sport is my passion.
I love sport! And Cape Town is good for so many sports because of the weather. I run every weekend with my dog, Oscar. I'm a member of the Sumner Running Club. We have the Boulders Beach 10 km run next Sunday. It's a great run with amazing views. In the summer, when it's windy, I go kitesurfing with my brother, Pete. It's fantastic fun. I sometimes go cycling with my friends, Kerry and Roger, on Sunday. We often cycle by the sea and watch the penguins.
Cape Town is just a beautiful place – great scenery, great weather and great food. I'm very lucky!

8.12 Who is it?

1 **Ben** Good morning Cape Town. How are you all on another lovely sunny day? This is Ben Smith on Radio Cape. Hello to our first caller this morning. It's Kate. Hi Kate! How are you today?
   Kate Hi Ben. I'm good, thanks. I'm so happy I'm on your radio show!

2 **Waiter** Good evening, everyone. Can I take your order?
   Ben Good evening. The oysters, please with a tomato salad.
   W Anything to drink?
   B Yeah! A beer, please.
   All Yeah – beers all round!

3 **Ben** Wow, Pete! It's so windy – look at the sea and the waves!
   Pete Yeah! It's a great day for it.
   B I'm ready! Let's go! Let's get down to the beach!

4 **Ben** Phew! Come on guys, we're nearly at the top!
   Roger Wow! Look at the view from here and look at the penguins!
   Kerry They're so funny!
   B They're great. I love watching them.

8.13 Directions

1 Go up the High Street. Turn right into Station Road. It's on the right, next to the Italian restaurant.
2 Go up the High Street. Turn right at the supermarket into Sandown Road, and it's on the left, next to the fish and chip shop.
3 Go up the High Street. Turn left at the church into Sandown Road. Go straight down, and turn right into Coastal Road. It's on the right, next to the Seaview Hotel.
4 Go straight on up the High Street for five minutes, and it's in Carden Square. It's a big building on the right.
5 Go up the High Street. Turn left into Station Road. Then turn right into Coastal Road and it's on the right, next to the Beach Café.
6 Go straight on up the High Street. Turn left into Dean Road and it's on your left, opposite the campsite.

Unit 10

10.1 Yesterday was Sunday

Kristin Yesterday I got up really late – about 10 o'clock. I had breakfast in bed – just orange juice, tea and toast – and I listened to music. I love doing this on Sunday. It was a beautiful morning, so I called my friend Max – he lives near me – and we went for walk in the park with his dog. Then we met some friends for coffee at a local café. It started to rain, so I invited my friends to my flat. I cooked a meal for them, just roast chicken and salad, and we stayed at home for the rest of the afternoon and watched a film. My friends left about 6 o'clock and I cleaned my flat and then went to bed early. I took my laptop to bed and did some work. I like working in bed because it's warm and comfortable, but I often fall asleep.

10.6 Kristin's weekend

K = Kristin, D = Dave

D What about you, Kristin? Did you have a good weekend?
K Oh yes, I did, very good.
D What did you do on Saturday?
K Well, on Saturday morning I went shopping and bought a new dress. Then on Saturday evening I went to a friend's party. It was fantastic!
D Who did you see at the party?
K Oh, lots of old friends and an old boyfriend. Good thing I bought the new dress! He looked awful, and I looked great!
D Did you get home late?
K Yes, I did. I didn't get up on Sunday until 10 o'clock and I had breakfast in bed.
D Wow, breakfast in bed! But it was a lovely day! I was on the golf course at 10 o'clock! So … What did you do after breakfast?
K Well, I was still very tired so I just called my friend Max and …
D Ah, your new boyfriend?
K He is not – we're just friends! Anyway, we went for a walk with his dog and met some friends for coffee, but then it started to rain.
D I know – we didn't play golf after lunch … What did you do in the afternoon?
K We all went back to my flat. I cooked lunch for everyone and we watched a film.
D Nice … Did you do anything on Sunday evening?
K Not much … I went to bed early, and I did some work in bed on my laptop.
D Hmm … I often work on my laptop in bed … but I always fall asleep.
K Me too. I didn't do much work at all.

10.9 Making conversation

1 A I went shopping yesterday.
   B Really? Where did you go?
   A Oxford Street.
   B Oh, lovely! What did you buy?
   A Well, I wanted a new dress for a friend's wedding, and I went to Selfridges.
   B Selfridges? Nice, but expensive! Did you find one?
   A Yes, I did. I found a beautiful blue one in the sale. It was only £65!
   B Wow! Well done!

2 A We went to that new Italian restaurant last night.
   B Mmm! What did you have?
   A Well, I had pasta and Tom had pizza.
   B Did you enjoy it?
   A Yes, it was excellent, and it wasn't expensive.

3 A We saw a lot of our friends in the coffee shop.
   B Oh! Who did you see?
   A Tessa and Rick and some other friends from work.
   B I don't think I know them.
   A They're really good fun!

4 A I played tennis at the weekend.
   B Oh, really? Where did you play?
   A In the park. It was lovely. It was so sunny.
   B What a great thing to do on a Sunday morning!

5 A The party on Saturday was great!
   B Oh good! What time did you leave?
   A Three in the morning. The music was fantastic!
   B Did you dance?
   A Of course! All night!

10.10 Gary and Cathy's holiday

C = Cathy, G = Gary

C Well, our main holiday is usually in winter.
G Yes, we don't like winter in England, so we usually go to Barbados in February for two lovely warm weeks, don't we, honey?
C Yes, we do – it's great! But last year we did something completely different. We didn't go away in winter – we had our main holiday in summer – and we went to the Ardèche in France!
G Yes, it was because we wanted to learn how to canoe …
C Well, you wanted to canoe. I wasn't so sure! You see in Barbados we just read and sunbathe, go swimming and …
G And in Barbados we always stay in a five-star hotel, and eat at expensive restaurants, but in France we stayed in a cabin on a campsite, and we cooked outside every night.
C Hmm, yes! Definitely not five-star food. But in fact I loved it! And I loved the canoeing, didn't I?
G You did. It was great fun.
C And Gary, you went fishing too, didn't you?
G We both went fishing!
C Well yes, but I didn't catch any fish. You caught a really big one!
G That's right. One of my best moments of the holiday. I usually play golf in Barbados, but I enjoyed the fishing more.
C And we met lots of lovely people, didn't we?
G We did. We made lots of new friends and had a really good time.
C And we always have a good time in Barbados, too, don't we?
G Yes, we're very lucky.

Unit 11

11.5 Bobby Boyd

Hi, my name's Bobby. I'm Irish, but I live in Lisbon, in Portugal. I teach English at a big school here. I can speak Portuguese fluently and German a little bit. I love it here. Most Saturdays I leave the city and go to Sintra. It's a beautiful old town very near Lisbon. I go with friends, and we usually go horse riding or walking in the lovely countryside. Sometimes we go surfing, too. The beaches are amazing. All my Portuguese friends can surf really well. I can't surf very well, so I sunbathe. I love the beaches here. On Sunday nights we sometimes go to Fado restaurants. Fado is traditional Portuguese music. I love it! I can now sing Fado quite well, but I can't play the guitar.
Sunday is also the day for 'sardinhas assadas' – grilled sardines in English. My friend, Jorge, always cooks delicious sardines with potatoes. I can't cook at all, but I sometimes make Irish coffee for my friends. Coffee, whiskey and cream! They love it, and so do I!

11.9 What do you do on your smartphone?

Keith, age 73

I play Scrabble with my son on my phone, I love it! I live in Scotland and my son lives in London. Playing Scrabble makes us feel nearby. We usually play in the evening after he finishes work. It is the best part of my day. I usually win! I had an eight-letter word yesterday and got eighty-two points!

Maddie, age 34

I'm a journalist – I work for the BBC. I travel a lot and take photos and videos of news events around the world on my phone and send them back to the BBC in London. It's amazing that I can send a video from Mumbai in India and it's on the 6 o'clock news! I use my phone 24/7, because news is 24/7!

Antonio, age 21

I'm Italian but I live and work in London at the moment. I miss my family so my phone is very important to me. Most evenings, when I finish work, I phone home. It's wonderful – I use FaceTime to see and speak to my family so I don't feel so sad. I can even see my dog, Clara. I speak to her and she knows my voice.

Kylie, age 17

The main thing I use my phone for is to message my friends. We text all the time, about everything in our lives, big and small. I often go on Facebook too – it's a great way to get everybody's news and we can share all our photos. Yesterday, we posted photos from this amazing party we went to last weekend. It was wild!

Josh, age 8

My mum and dad say I can use my phone after school and homework, and sometimes at the weekend. Mostly I play games on it with my friends. My favourite game is Flappy Birds. It's great fun, I love it! We have big competitions – I win a lot, not always of course, but most times.

Taylor, age 42

I work for a large global company. I work long hours and I travel a lot. My phone is very important for work - I can arrange meetings and talk to clients when I'm on the train. And I send and receive emails. But every weekend, when I can, I turn my phone off and just spend time with my wife and two young daughters. My job is important to me, but my family is too.

🔊 11.10 Adjectives and nouns

1   A   A Ferrari is a fantastic car. It's very fast.
    B   Yeah, I know, but it's also so expensive.
2   A   We can't go for a walk – it's too cold and wet.
    B   Yes, we can. Look it's sunny again! Come on!
3   A   How tall is your brother?
    B   He's very tall – 1.9 metres. I'm only 1.7 metres.
4   A   I think motor racing is a really dangerous sport.
    B   I know it's dangerous, but it's exciting too. That's why I love it!
5   A   Can I have a fresh orange juice, please?
    B   I'm afraid we don't have fresh.
    A   OK. Just a glass of water then.
6   A   New York is a very cosmopolitan city. I love it.
    B   Me, too. I can't believe I'm here.
7   A   Charlie Chaplin made some very funny films, don't you think?
    B   No, I don't like his films. I think they're really boring.

Unit 12

🔊 12.3 Where is Harry?

1   **H = Harry, T = Tariq**

    H   Good morning, Tariq. I'd like *The Times* and this month's car magazine.
    T   Morning, Harry. Is that all?
    H   Yes, that's all. Oh, I'd like a birthday card, too. It's my mum's birthday tomorrow.
    T   The cards are next to you.
    H   Hmm. This one looks OK.
    T   Would you like a bag?
    H   No, thanks. I don't need a bag.
    T   That's £6.50.

2   **W = Woman, H = Harry**

    W   Can I help you?
    H   Good afternoon. I'd like to post this parcel, please.
    W   Can you put it on the scales? That's one kilo exactly! Would you like to send it first or second class?
    H   First, please. It's a birthday present for my mum and it's her birthday tomorrow!
    W   That's OK. We can do that.
    H   Phew!
    W   Anything else?
    H   That's it, thanks.

🔊 12.6 Birthday wishes

Jill

What would I like for my birthday? That's easy! I'd like to have breakfast in bed. With my favourite magazine. And in the evening I'd like to go to a restaurant with my husband. I don't mind if it's Italian, French, Chinese or English. Just good food, my husband and no children!

Sammy

Well, I'd like a new laptop, because my laptop is so old and all the new software doesn't work on it. And then in the evening I'd like to go to the cinema. I'd like to see a really good action movie with fast cars!

Zoe

I'd love some trainers. White ones, please. My old ones are OK for running but I'd love some new white ones. And in the evening I'd like to go dancing with all my friends and have a great time.

🔊 12.8 *like* and *would like*

1   A   What would you like? Would you like a Coke?
    B   Yes, please. I'm very thirsty.
2   A   What sort of thing do you like doing at the weekend?
    B   Well, I like watching films.
3   A   What sort of house do you want to move into?
    B   We'd like a house with a big kitchen. Somewhere near the centre of town.
4   A   We have this weekend free. What would you like to do?
    B   I'd like to have the weekend with you, and only you!
    A   Oooh!
5   A   What do you spend all your money on?
    B   Well, I like new clothes. I buy new clothes every week.

Unit 13

🔊 13.10 Opposite verbs in conversation

1   A   Would you like an espresso?
    B   No, thank you, I hate black coffee.
    A   Do you? I love it.
2   A   What time does the film start?
    B   6.45.
    A   And do you know when it finishes?
    B   About 8.30, I think.
3   A   Would you like to play tennis after work?
    B   Sorry, I can't. I'm working late again.
4   A   Our train leaves London at 13.55.
    B   And what time does it arrive in Paris?
    A   16.05.
    B   Wow! That's fast.
5   A   Did you remember to bring your dictionary?
    B   Oh, sorry. I forgot it.
    A   Not again!
6   A   Can I open the window? I'm hot.
    B   Of course. Just remember to close it when you leave the room.

Unit 14

🔊 14.4 Where are they?

S = Stewart, G = Geoff

1   G   This music is great. Come on, let's dance!
    S   We have an early start tomorrow, Geoff, and it's one o'clock in the morning!
    G   Come on, Stewart. We're on holiday. One more dance.
    S   OK then. Just one more.
2   S   Bye bye, England! Spain, here we come!
    G   Ugh! I feel awful. How long are we on this ferry?
    S   Only 12 hours. You'll be fine.
    G   Oh no! 12 hours. Where's the bathroom?
3   G   Mmm! These tapas are delicious.
    S   The best! I really like the chorizo sausage one.
    G   More sangria?
    S   Yes please. Salud!
    G   Salud!
4   G   Wow! This port is over two thousand years old! It really is an old port!
    S   It's a really cool place. There are lots of lovely bars and restaurants, too. Hey, Geoff! How about a beer in Le Bar de la Marine?
    G   Good idea, Stew! How's your French?
    S   Awful!